AF585078

Wakefield Press

Never Carry Your Own Briefcase

Never Carry Your Own Briefcase

John M. Allgrove

Wakefield
Press

Wakefield Press
16 Rose Street
Mile End
South Australia 5031
www.wakefieldpress.com.au

First published 2015

Edited by Molly Jureidini, Wakefield Press
Cover designed by J. Marc Allgrove
Text designed and typeset by Wakefield Press
Printed in Australia by Ligare Pty Ltd

National Library of Australia Cataloguing-in-Publication entry

Creator:	Allgrove, John M., author.
Title:	Never carry your own briefcase / John M. Allgrove.
ISBN:	978 1 74305 366 9 (hardback).
Subjects:	Allgrove, John.
	Australian Trade Commissioner Service.
	Government employees – Australia – Biography.
	Civil service – Australia – Biography.
	Australia – Officials and employees – Foreign countries.
Dewey Number:	352.63092

To

Maureen, my much loved wife

and

David (dec), Anne-Marie, Marc and Benjamin.

A family of whom I am so, so proud.

Contents

Prologue		*1*
CHAPTER ONE	Calcutta and Bombay, India	*10*
CHAPTER TWO	Cairo, Egypt	*31*
CHAPTER THREE	Hong Kong, Hong Kong	*43*
CHAPTER FOUR	Taipei, Taiwan	*48*
CHAPTER FIVE	Bangkok, Thailand	*57*
CHAPTER SIX	Paris, France	*68*
CHAPTER SEVEN	Jakarta, Indonesia	*88*
CHAPTER EIGHT	Seoul, South Korea	*100*
CHAPTER NINE	Frankfurt, Germany	*108*
CHAPTER TEN	Singapore, Singapore	*114*
Epilogue		*127*

Prologue

I was born on 24 October 1932 to Joseph William Allgrove and Marjorie (née Walden) in the General Hospital, Johor Bahru. Father was a rubber planter, the estate where he was manager being located near Segamat in the state of Johor. At the time, Johor was one of the Federation of States of Malaysia, a British colony.

Memories are vivid of the open two-storey home set in large gardens, surrounded by row upon row of rubber trees. Burst of colour against a sea of green. Hibiscus, frangipani, morning glory and gloriosa creepers, vivid red and purple bougainvillea and coloured palms, amongst others, that together provided a rainbow of colours. An overall vision of lushness.

The Chinese amah, immaculate in her baggy black pants and starched white blouse buttoned at the neck was ever present, only 'handing me back' to Father and Mother at mealtimes and before going to bed. Loyal protective servants glided around performing their various responsibilities in return, not only for a wage, but also housing, food, medical care and schooling for their children.

Wood-fired stove, kerosene refrigerator, only overhead fans for cooling, mosquito nets in bedrooms, and a mosquito-proof room where pre- and after-dinnertime was spent. A pre-dinner whisky was father's usual (called a *stengah* – Scotch and soda!). Bathrooms contained a large pottery tub filled with cold water from which one used a dipper to throw water over oneself – soap up and then repeat the process to rinse off. A hot tub was unknown!

Supplies of frozen meat, butter, cheese, only powdered milk was available, tinned food, groceries, and pharmacy requirements were delivered by train once a week from Singapore. Fresh fruit and vegetables were available locally. Bananas, pawpaw, green oranges, mangosteens, rambutans, limes, coconuts and pineapples were delicious. Temperate climate fruits were rarely available.

Very early years passed quickly. The overall regime of a planter was a term of four years, followed by nine months leave which included the sea journey to and from the UK. Any child of six or seven years at the time of their parents' leave would be left at boarding school in the UK, not to see their mother or father for the next four years! In September 1937, when just short of five years of age, I was placed in a boarding school in the Cameron Highlands, north of Kuala Lumpur, and saw my parents three times a year at each of the three end-of-term holidays. No weekends (exeats) at home.

That first away-from-home experience began at 1 am one dark morning when I was shaken awake by parents who then, with me still in my pyjamas, drove to the local station to meet the 'school train' on its way to Kuala Lumpur from Singapore, picking up 'sons and daughters' on the journey. The night was dark and wet and the platform had few lights. Out of the dark the steam engine appeared. Stopping only briefly. One carriage door opened and a very British female teacher called out: 'Are you there, Allgrove?' I was four years, ten months old! Handed over to this complete stranger, the door slammed shut and, mildly terrified, I was shown to a bunk with the suggestion that I should go to sleep. Kuala Lumpur was seven hours away. Cameron Highlands was even further. I didn't see my parents for three months – no phone calls, perhaps an odd postcard and obviously no email, YouTube, Facebook, Twitter or Skype facilities.

The British were brutal with their children, not physically of course, but who would stand for this introduction to one's child's education today.

There were however many good memories – there needed to be! Walks in the main forest, wonderful birds and butterflies, encounters with the indigenous Dyaks, who impressed with their skill with a blowpipe when hunting. Rushing streams and waterfalls, and flowers in abundance. I loved the voracious insect-devouring pitcher plants.

By the age of seven I knew where natural rubber came from, how it was 'tapped', collected, coagulated in large tanks (a little like milk, cheese and whey), rolled into sheets, cured in a smokehouse, baled and shipped overseas to the Dunlops, Goodyears, and Michelins of this world. The large Japanese tyre manufacturers were not known then, or at least to a seven-year-old English boy being brought up in one of Britain's colonies.

Looking back now, and against the background of society today, what a regime that young children of parents working in the colonies were subjected to. Looked after and cared for largely by others, but initially totally devoid of experiencing the joy of participating in family life.

In September 1939 the dark clouds of war had started forming over Europe and my parents leave couldn't be spent in England, so the question arose: 'Where to go for leave?' Australia was chosen, but first my sister Jane, four years my senior, had to be brought from England to Singapore, having already been left at boarding school on the previous parental leave.

With Adelaide as the ultimate destination, we all embarked on the MV *Charon* bound for Fremantle via Derby and Broome on the coast of Western Australia. We couldn't believe our eyes when the tide went out and left the ship high and dry whilst in Broome. Just had to wait until the tide came back in before sailing on to Fremantle. Then by train to Adelaide. What a contrast! From the lush greens of the tropics to the brown barren lands of the Nullarbor Plain. The actual carriages of the train are now on show at the National Train Museum at Port Adelaide. Worth a visit.

A house was rented in Wayville and I was enrolled at St Peter's College, Jane at Walford. There we remained for the rest of our primary and secondary education.

Leave soon ran out and in mid 1940 Dad and Mum returned to

Muar River Estate – Jane and I staying in Adelaide as boarders. We were left under the guardianship of Percy and Bryce Andrews, who together with their two children, Barbara and Bruce, took us into their home for what was to be five long years. A gesture of love and caring, which will never be forgotten, especially the many weekends spent at their shack, a converted railway carriage off Hallett Road, Burnside, and Christmas holidays in Port Elliot.

Pearl Harbor in December 1941 signalled the beginning of a major change in our lives. Mother was killed when leaving Singapore by sea, just before its fall in February 1942, and Father spent the rest of the war, until August 1945, helping, along with thousands of others, to build the bridge over the River Kwai and the associated railway from Thailand to Burma.

After his release, and spending several months establishing beyond doubt that Mother had died, Dad returned to Adelaide to hopefully reunite with his children he had last seen five years earlier.

For him, after what he had been through, the miracle happened. We were at the old Adelaide airport at Parafield to greet him as he stepped off the plane.

Recovery was remarkably swift and an accidental meeting in King William Street with Nell Hannah, one of the survivors of the Bangka Massacre of Australian nurses by the Japanese (refer to the film *Paradise Road*), turned into a lifelong relationship. Married in Singapore on 16 December 1946, a family soon followed, Jeremy in October 1948, Jessica in September 1950 and Jeffrey in January 1953.

By early 1946 Dad had returned to Muar River Estate, and immediately set about rebuilding the house, a rubber plantation, factory and facilities for several hundred estate workers. A daunting and highly emotional task, which he accomplished with Nell's very able assistance. Where matters of workers (tappers) housing, health and education were concerned she was highly skilled and dedicated.

My first visit to Muar River Estate after the war was during the summer school holidays of 1947–1948. Accompanied by Jane, we again travelled by sea from Perth to Singapore and then by car across the causeway and through Johor to Segamat – the nearest provincial town to the estate.

First impressions were how little had changed. One was unaware of the mood of the people and how it was slowly evolving. Some elements were planning independence and the Communist insurgents – who had fought from the jungle hideouts against the Japanese throughout the latter's brutal occupation – now turned their thoughts towards getting rid of the British and establishing a Communist state.

What became known as the Emergency began in May 1948 and continued until 1960. Many planters were killed, as well as many more ethnic Malays, Chinese and Indians. Not until the Resettlement Program was introduced were Chin Peng and his Vietcong-like fighters flushed out of their jungle hideouts, finally fleeing to southern Thailand. Separation of Singapore from Malaya followed and with it full independence for Malaya.

This whole period is a fascinating story in itself, the most notable feature being that if the wives of planters hadn't stayed with their men, the battle would almost certainly have been lost, and Malaya would have fallen under the Red Tide.

Further visits followed in the summers of 1948–1949 and 1950–1951, when the situation was very volatile and not conducive to enjoying a holiday as movement was severely restricted and always accompanied by an armed escort. With extensive roadside cover (jungle and rubber plantations), ambushes were very common.

The protected life at boarding school (1940–1950), with exeats and holidays spent at the homes of other boarders, and of course the Andrews, came to an end, following which it was out 'into the real world'. For this I was not really prepared, especially as one felt 'afloat' with no home base.

The year 1951 saw employment for a time as a cadet with Shell Company and then as a travelling salesman with a company that sold cotton and linen products direct to families in the country. Neither worked out. In 1952 I enrolled in the Agricultural Science Faculty of Adelaide University, at the end of year one going to England to complete my degree at Reading University.

The years at Reading were full of student activity, including the development of a love of rugby union football – which continues today – and, of course, some study! This concluded with a Bachelor of Agricultural Science degree. I returned to Australia towards the end of 1956, a decision accelerated by the deepening Suez crisis, which saw moves to have me conscripted into the British Army. I got out just in time.

My best friend, Donald G. Daw, met me on arrival and said that he had an interview arranged for a position with Swift & Co. I was successful and remained with the company, initially in Adelaide and then in Head Office, Sydney, until joining the Australian Trade Commissioner Service in mid 1961.

My first posting was to Calcutta, India in May 1962. It is from here that the 'Never Carry Your Own Briefcase' story begins.

PS The account that my father wrote outlining all that he was able to ascertain as to my mother's final days, is quoted here.

> Dear John,
> The following is all I know of Mummy's last week or so. I have written it out for you, Jane and a few of our relations. You may like to have it when you're older and for the present I'll keep it for you. I wrote this on Armistice Day 1945.
>
> With love,
>
> Dad
>
> Mummy left to go to Singapore a day or two after war broke out in Malaya. Volunteers were required for nursing in various hospitals – she thought she should offer her services. The first arrangement was that she should go to Alexandra Hospital, and she started a brief training in straight forward nursing, giving injections etc.

An auxiliary hospital was started at St Andrew's School, which was entirely taken over for medical purposes. Someone was wanted to supervise the supply and preparation of food for patients and staff. As this was a job Mummy could take on immediately she was shipped over to St Andrew's. It seemed a better thing in every way, as besides being a job where she was of more use, Mummy could live in Sorby Adams' house on the same site.

The work was strenuous. The number of patients varied almost hour by hour – air raid wardens and casualties, AID wounded, Penang evacuees, convalescent troops, and later, wounded came and went daily. With increasing danger of bombing, Asiatic staff became more difficult to retain, although the regular house staff were strong and loyal. Food became more and more difficult to procure, but somehow supplies were maintained.

All this time Mummy kept up more than her normal correspondence. Her one fear was of being sent somewhere other than Malaya or Australia – fear of not being able to look after the family if her job were taken away for any reason. She has written more than once to me, saying that the other European women intended to stay on if she did. If she wasn't, they were all going. Sister Simmons and Mrs Kathleen Lim, Miss Thomas and Mrs Fass were the others, Mrs Waddle and Mrs Wilson had gone, each having small children.

On 19 February I was with the J.V.E. in slit trenches around Draycott House, about two miles north of Singapore town. A company of A.I.F. were on our left and an Australian twenty-five-pounder battery in the ravine below us. About 5 pm someone gave a shout that I was wanted up on the road. Mummy had driven out to see me. She wasn't a bit scared and the Aussies gave her a cheer. She came out to say that they were alright and the hospital, no one had been hurt by bombing, but constant supervision was necessary to keep up the supply of meals. (She remembered to bring the razor blades, soap etc.) She intended to stay on unless forced to leave by government. Then she drove back.

On 11 February (Thursday) she came out again, about the same time, with the news that all government sisters were to concentrate at Government House for evacuations, but no instructions had been made for the voluntary workers. Then I made the fatal mistake of telling her to get on the first boat possible. And so, off she went – still smiling.

We were on guard alternative hours, day and night, expecting an attack at any time. On one day, I forget exactly which, we were informed that we had to hang on for a few days only, as the Americans had landed in the West Coast. Port Swettenham and Port Dickson were mentioned. We didn't believe even then that Singapore would fall, despite the fact that various troops retreated back through our lines.

On Saturday 14 February I got two hours leave to go down and make enquiries, the second-in-command Captain Cross (who died in Thailand), lending me his car. I went straight to St Andrew's which was being evacuated. I saw Sorby Adams who assured me that the European women had got away by boat the morning before – Friday 13 February. I went back to our lines quite satisfied that they were alright.

I heard nothing more whatsoever until I returned to Singapore on 23 September 1945. Harry Ward and I got into Singapore from our reception camp at the 12th Mile Change Road pretty late that evening. The Recovered Allied Prisoners of War and Internees Organisation could not help me much with my inquiries, only assuring me that they had no information of prisoner of war records. Colin Yang, who had been at Penang, and thence came to Singapore in 1942 and was at St Andrews. He had a note in his diary confirming that Mummy left Singapore on the evening of 12 February or morning of 13 February. He suggested I see Dr Elliot – an old friend of ours, with whom Mrs Lim had stayed until the day I arrived in Singapore. Mrs Lim was the last of the people we knew who saw Mummy. It was too late to see Dr Elliot then. She is a wonderful person – worked as MO of St Andrew's Medical Mission for many years, and was interned in Singapore throughout the war. She is white, frail and bent now, but full of good spirits and pluck, so I got in again the next morning and arranged to go to Cathedral House in the afternoon. She had Kathleen Lim's story (since repeated to me by Sorby Adams). They left Singapore on the 'Gran Bee'. Just before dusk the ship was attacked by Japanese planes. Mummy was wounded in the back by the first bomb. She was in considerable pain, but able to walk. Mrs Lim was put in one (life) boat and saw her going towards a different boat. Mrs Lim got to Sumatra and made inquiries for Mummy at once. There was never any information forthcoming and the inference is that the other boat was sunk when the Japanese machine gunned them as they left the ship. Sister Simmons also was never heard of again.

Mrs Lim was interned in Sumatra, returned to Penang at the instigation of her husband (a Chinese), re-taken by the Japs, both interned in Singapore. She survived, and is back in Penang.

This is the best I can do. I have written this out on 8 November 1945.

Dad

CHAPTER ONE

Calcutta and Bombay, India

1962–1963

Post included responsibilities for Australia's trade interests in Burma.

Pre-departure story
When: early 1962 in Canberra.
Location: Common Room provided for trade commissioners visiting Canberra between postings and trainee TCs, I being one, prior to embarking on their first assignment overseas.
Time: End of the day when the above would gather, get to know each other, exchange experiences and usually have a beer, or two!

Meeting for the first time a rather round, receding hairline TC with a somewhat 'plum in the mouth' English accent – one Duncan McPhee. I was asked if I had been advised of where my posting was to be.

'Calcutta,' I responded.

'Oh, Calcutta – yes.' Expecting a mine of information to follow as he advised that he had spent a posting in Calcutta, I waited to hang on to every word, primarily responses to the many questions I wished to ask. Instead: 'Allgrove, just one thing to remember when in Calcutta, indeed in India, never carry your own briefcase!'

Not another word of advice or general information followed. To this day I have never seen the said gentleman again.

Scheduled to arrive in May 1962, the hottest month of the year in Calcutta. The four-engined Qantas Constellation touched down in Dum Dum Airport at midnight.

In the arrivals area I was met by Moorthy, the office driver. Once out of the airport – so named because of the nearby munitions factory that amongst other ordinance, produced the infamous hollow-nosed lead rifle shell named the 'dum-dum' bullet – the stifling heat was all enveloping. When questioned as to why he was carrying a heavy stick, Moorthy replied: 'Rabid dogs very bad, Sahib!' This, added to the many very large flying cockroaches that flew at me as I walked to the car and clung onto one's clothing, made for an uncomfortable arrival.

The aroma of dried cattle dung fuelled fires in clay cooking pots, remained an ever-present invasion of my nostrils throughout my stay in India.

Lined up to meet me on arrival at the ground floor apartment, at what was now almost 0200 hours, were those who were to care for me over the months ahead.

Lachme (bearer)

Mummil (cook)

Sibu (sweeper)

Mahanty (gardener)

In addition, the cost of a night watchman (*durwan*) and clothes washer (*dhobi*), was shared with the occupants of the two other apartments, each being a whole floor, one above the other. Before one questions the number of servants, one has to realise and understand that each had very specific duties, an inevitable division of labour, ensuring that six people would earn at least something to support their families. Needless to say wages were very low.

Moorthy picked me up the next morning for my first day in the office. As was the custom, I sat in the back. On arrival Moorthy quickly came round and opened the kerb-side door. I emerged with my briefcase. Wrong!

'Sahib, please never carry your own briefcase, I will bring it up to your office!'

From then on I decided that if I were to put pen to paper and write my memoirs, then the title would be as it is.

Normal day dress for the office was white shirt, shorts or trousers. Many pairs were required because one often changed two or three times a day due to the sweat-inducing heat. So priority number one on my first day at the office was to visit the tailor, one Shaik Sillar, who had 'dressed' many of my predecessors. First question was, 'Good morning, Sahib, please, on which side do you dress?' I hadn't been faced by that question before. Suffice to say it only applies and is specific to the male of the human species! The rest I'll leave to your imagination, but it does make a difference!

The Trade Commission office in Calcutta was situated on the third floor of a building owned and occupied by one of the several, but already diminishing number of British agency houses. The days of the Raj were clearly in decline. Only three offices (that of the TC, the ATC and their shared secretary), were air conditioned, the rest of the staff being spread across a large open-plan area with overhead fans (*punkas*). Often though the latter were to be desired, because the air conditioner vents in our offices continuously spat out a variety of insects, mainly cockroaches, onto one's desk!

How differently an office was staffed in India, compared with Australia, was very apparent when one considers jobs/responsibility.

Titles	*Nationality*
Trade Commissioner (1)	Australian
Assistant TC (1)	Australian
Joint Private Secretary (1)	British
Marketing Officer (1)	Indian
Chief Clerk (1)	Indian
Accountant/Paymaster (1)	Indian
Senior Stenographer for MO (1)	Indian
Trade Enquiry Clerk (1)	Indian
Records Clerk (1)	Indian
Junior Stenographer (1)	Indian
Librarian (1)	Indian
Telephonist/Receptionist (1)	Indian
Office Driver (1)	Indian
Messengers (4)	Indian
Sweeper (cleaner) (1)	Indian

Wow! Eighteen in total. Division of labour existed even more so in offices than in the home. An era many years before the advent of computers.

The Bengal Club remained one of the surviving bastions of the Raj. Its impressive facade, large entrance hall, and sweeping staircase dividing at the top led to the dining, smoking and reading rooms and other facilities and an area for large functions. Tall, immaculately dressed staff, largely from northern India, addressed the every need of members, generally from the vantage point made possible by their height – exceeding two metres when their turbans were included. Within a week of arrival in Calcutta, a long-time resident invited me to lunch. I was advised it would be discourteous to refuse. When passing the Reading Room on departure from an excellent meal, I noticed a member sprawled back in an armchair, legs supported by arms that swung out for this purpose, with a copy of the *London*

Financial Times open across his chest. Eyes closed, fast asleep. What drew my attention was a staff member seemingly writing something on the soles of his shoes.

Enquiring of my host resulted in: 'Oh! With a piece of chalk he's writing the time when he should wake the dormant member!' At least in the Bengal Club, Calcutta, the days of the Raj were very much alive!

Golf at the Tollygunge Club had an unusual twist. Two aides for each player – one caddy to carry the clubs, the other an *argi wallah* (ball boy) to go down the fairway ahead of the shot played to mark where the ball stopped or to find a lost ball. Betting amongst these (eight for each foursome) was fierce, betting of course on the player's longest drive, number of shots for the hole etc.

Cheating was rampant. For example, a bad lie was often corrected by the *argi wallah* unnoticeably stepping on his player's ball, holding it between his toes and quietly dropping it on a more favourable lie without anyone noticing – not even the player! For expatriates in Calcutta, the Tollygunge Club, together with the swimming, cricket, rugby and tennis clubs, were the centres of one's social and recreational life. They provided facilities for golf, horseracing, swimming, tennis, cricket, soccer, and rugby, as well as dining, bar etc.

In all of my thirty-four years spent overseas in the service, Calcutta was the only posting where, on two occasions when meeting a visiting Australian businessman on arrival at Dum Dum Airport and starting the almost hour-long drive into the city, I was asked to go back to the airport. The poverty, the smells all became too much, even in such a short time after arrival.

Calcutta, the capital of West Bengal, at that time was a city of almost nine million. Situated on the banks of the Hooghly River, this being one of principal outlet tributaries of the mighty Ganges River, it was a State of some forty-eight million – of which 10,000–11,000 were Europeans (6000–7000 British). Australians numbered some seventy, based on those who were registered.

Cholera, smallpox, malaria, dengue fever, dysentery and typhoid were all endemic, sometimes reaching epidemic levels. One soon learnt the importance of eating only with the right hand, the left being reserved for the needs of toilet activity! Very necessary to know, because in the country especially, the use of knife and fork was often not an option.

Whilst English was widely spoken, almost always with that familiar accent, or at least understood, there were many amusing exchanges resulting from the choice and order of words used. One example. A sign in the lobby of a hotel: 'The manager has personally passed all the water served here.'

However, other than Hong Kong and Singapore, India for an English-speaking foreigner was in many ways the easiest to come to grips with. A democracy based on the UK system of administration, enormously frustrating, but understood because of its operating systems prior to independence. This applied throughout the banking, power, rail, postal, air and other public utility providers. Very different when working in, say, Indonesia, Taiwan, South Korea or even France and Germany, which were to follow.

An interesting real-life example of the variety that the English language can provide is contained in the following letter I received from my next-door neighbour in Calcutta very soon after arrival.

To
Mr Dotsan,
The Deputy Trade Commissioner,
Australia.
11/1, Alipore Avenue,
Calcutta 27.

Dear Sir,

I most reluctantly bring to your kind notice the following facts for information and favour of taking such action as you deem proper.

My building is situated just opposite your house at 44/16, Durgapur Lane. At least a dozen of ladies are inmates. The male folk of the house all go out during the day time to earn their livelihood.

During noon time, these ladies – some of them are young and some unmarried – became victims of your people, who by their vulgar and ungentlemanly gestures, have made a veritable hell of the lives of these girls. The poor ladies have become very much frightened and ashamed at such behaviour – they can not go on the roof to dry their clothes, they can not go to the balcony to air themselves. They have to shut their windows the whole day to save them from the onslaught of your people. A man called Shiboo, who perhaps lives in the southern side of the first floor, is ringleader.

After waiting for a long time I have no other alternative but to approach you to intervene personally so that these sorry state of affairs may be stopped forthwith.

Yours faithfully,
Sm* (Nivanani Das)
44/16, Durgapur Lane, Cal – 27.

* *Abbreviation for Srimati (Mrs)*

Not sure where the Mr Dotsan came from. Not remotely representative of my name unless one takes a long bow – Mr Dotsan/Mr John? Shiboo named as the culprit was in fact Sibu, my sweeper.

India was a nation with such a rich history and traditions, some of the latter creating a major obstacle to development. An enormous gap existed between the relatively few rich, some very rich, and the many desperately poor – the slums of Calcutta and Bombay are shattering in their extent and the obvious poverty of those who live there. During my period of posting I, at the request of the Save the Children Fund Branch of Victoria, monitored the use of funds that the organisation provided for the operation of a children's creche in the heart of what I describe as Mother Theresa country. Ensuring the funds were distributed as intended and not siphoned off by corrupt officials was the principal task. The faces and smiles of these children will remain with me forever.

In vivid contrast was the lifestyle of the privileged few who lived in large, garden-surrounded homes within walled and guarded compounds with many servants. To obtain, and indeed convey, a feel of India in the early 1960s, is not an easy task. Perhaps best approached by just a few stories.

The bovine of the species, the cow, is sacred in India. In rural areas there are few problems experienced because of this, but in the cities the impact can be very significant. Cows cannot be moved from any site on which they choose to be – standing, feeding, lying down, whatever. In practical terms this means, that if a cow wanders into a market and starts feeding from sacks of grain, the often impoverished stall or shop holder can do nothing but watch his produce disappear. Sleeping across the entrance to a building often causes a problem. 'Step over me if you can, but don't try to move me and risk the wrath of the passing public if you dare touch or hit me', is the cow's message to all who pass by. The biggest black bull regularly spread himself across the entrance to the building that housed the Trade Commissioner's office. One had to pass by with the greatest care.

The fear instilled by a Calcutta mob in full flight is impossible to convey in words. I experienced this once when returning from a visit to the children's creche. The reason for the rioting thousands was never to be known. Could well have been a domestic issue, maybe a Hindu/Muslim minor slur that set the confrontation off to its uncontrollable end. Only quick thinking by my driver enabled us to flee the area.

Although sectarian conflicts are relatively rare within India today – as opposed to the major international differences, e.g. the issue of Kashmir between Hindu India and Muslim Pakistan – vivid memories of partition were very apparent in the 1960s.

When East Bengal became Bangladesh there was a massive movement of Hindus towards Calcutta and a comparable movement of Muslims from Bengal to Bangladesh. During my stay in Calcutta I received many horrifying reports of train loads of people passing each way with the train being stopped at the border (whether going east or west), and Muslim mobs decapitating Hindus going west and the same happening to Muslims proceeding east. For decades during British Colonial rule these people had lived happily side by side.

In sharp contrast I was deeply moved by the following 'poem' by a sixteen-year-old student at the Baramati High School, Baramati, a small village south-east of Bombay soon after one passes through Poona.

'What is Life?'

Life is a gift	accept it
Life is a challenge	meet it
Life is an adventure	dare it
Life is a promise	fulfil it
Life is a game	play it
Life is a mystery	unfold it
Life is a puzzle	solve it
Life is a song	sing it
Life is a goal	achieve it
Life is a journey	complete it

What a perceptive philosophical view of life by such a young mind surrounded by so much hardship and poverty that is prevalent in this large vibrant country.

There were many examples of what I saw as innocent decadence by Europeans living in India, though in part understood as being a counter to the harsh, at least climatic, conditions under which they lived – not exactly the soft green fields of rural England or indeed the leafy suburbs of Adelaide!

One such experience was enjoyed if one was invited to stay on after one of the many cocktail parties hosted by Marge and Joe Lever, manager of the Hong Kong and Shanghai Bank. Such an invitation was conveyed by a whisper in the ear during the course of the evening!

The setting was around, and indeed mainly in, the swimming

pool, garden lights in the trees and on one of Calcutta's very frequently occurring hot and humid evenings. Costumes were provided, and as one immersed oneself up to the neck, bearers would walk up and down with silver trays on which an array of ice-cold drinks were arranged – beer, gin and tonic and the most favoured Scotch on the rocks, or with a liberal splash of soda. 'Excuse me, Sahib, drink, Sahib?'

Another 'fun' experience was that of rickshaw races after rugby on a Saturday evening. Post-match consumption of a serious number of beers often led to a rickshaw race challenge between players. Into the streets outside the ground we would venture, fairly vocally, and each participant would hail one of the numerous rickshaws on the street. The owner would be put in the seat, the rugby player took up the shafts. Then, arranged up to ten abreast, we would wait for the starting signal. People, cars and dogs got out of the way, often ungraciously, as the race ran its course, often concluding with not very serious crashes between participants. Owners would gesticulate loudly, demanding a 'fare' for the use of rickshaws and compensation for any damage inflicted on the only asset they possessed. The amount was the subject of intense bargaining, a settlement always being reached.

One could never get away from the abject poverty of so many. When there, it was estimated that at any given time, over two million people were born, grew up, procreated and died on the streets of Calcutta, without ever having a roof over their head. At dusk it was almost impossible to walk on any footpath that ran past a building with an overhanging verandah. Masses would position themselves for the night under the cover provided. If that could be alongside a friendly cow for warmth during the winter months, so much the better.

One day when at Calcutta market, a young boy, obviously very hungry, tugged at my trousers begging for money. Knowing that acceding would not benefit him at all – he was simply a tool for an adult who was watching from a distance – I took him by the hand, sat him on the kerb by a milk bar, bought a pint of milk and handed it to him. His sucking on the straw was continuous, without breath, and soon the bottle was drained. I'm unlikely to ever forget the look in his eyes. If God can show gratitude for a friendly act, then he certainly did so then through those dark wonderful eyes. Within a matter of seconds I was set upon by a very agitated and angry woman – the watching adult that wanted money. Fortunately several bystanders had observed proceedings and they attacked this hapless person, who managed to break away. The last I ever saw of her was her flailing legs disappearing in the crowd with several in pursuit!

Incidentally, Calcutta Market was, at that time, the largest market in the world under one roof. At one end merchants sold all manner of pots and pans, then there was the cloth section, fabrics from all over India of varying quality. So it progressed through groceries, grains, vegetables and fruit, meat (ugh!), furniture, pharmaceuticals etc. etc. until finally one came to the live animal section. Chickens and fish, a wide variety of wildlife of all shapes and sizes, even an elephant! All there to be purchased.

Driving was a hazardous occupation. For this reason, as a European, one benefited by having a driver, though I didn't except during working hours. Accidents were frequent and people would often throw themselves at the side of the car, in front was too dangerous, and when one stopped the uninjured individual would demand money. Women with a deformed child would approach the car when stationary at traffic lights, or just held up because of the crowd, bang on the window, again demanding money. Sadly many children were maimed just for this purpose. Another common 'trick' was to bandage a child's eyes and the outstretched hand of the beggar would claim that the often-screaming child was blind. Removal of the bandage would reveal that biting insects had been placed around the eyelids, obviously to induce, at the very least, acute irritation. No wonder the child screamed.

What a complex country. The caste system, arranged marriages, strict protocols to which women had to adhere, the myriad of specific gods from which a family may consider a particular god more important than another (resulting in many more public holidays in India than are customary in Australia), and the sacred position of the cow, completed the kaleidoscope of protocols in this colourful, complicated country.

The reality of India was only really experienced in rural areas. Within the major cities (Calcutta, New Delhi, Bombay, Madras and Bangalore, to name a few), although each have desperately poor slum areas, the CBD of each had obvious signs of mimicking the Western world. Modern shops and hotels, neon signs, increasing numbers of cars competing in a chaotic manner with bicycles and rickshaws and of course pedestrians going this and every way like ants.

Fortunately my early years in an Asian environment made it easy for me to approach this, my first posting, with a completely open mind and realising, and accepting, that India had an enormously rich and complex history stretching over hundreds of years – compared with the two hundred or so years of European settlement in Australia. Clearly it would be essential to recognise and appreciate that 'success in Asia' normally requires a significantly different approach to that which one would adopt in Australia.

One example was the differences in the concept of time required to develop relationships and subsequently conclude a contract. The building of a human relationship was an integral part of concluding a deal. In most instances it was more, or as important, as a signed contract – the latter seldom being of any value unless the personal relationship was sound. In the event of a dispute, recourse was often very difficult and costly to pursue, with any consequent arbitration being according to the rules and procedures of the local regime.

Travel out of Calcutta was infrequent, difficult for any extended period, and largely unnecessary as all meaningful contacts, and hence decisions, were made in Calcutta for industries within the region.

Visits to Durgapur steel mills and coalmines required driving north along the Grand Trunk Road, made famous by Rudyard Kipling, and remains the most unnerving experience I've ever had. Speeding coal trucks feeding Calcutta's power stations, bullock carts, bicycles and pedestrian traffic along the fringes of the narrow road all caused traffic chaos. One barely went five kilometres without seeing an overturned vehicle in the paddy (rice) fields, which stretched endlessly in each direction.

A planned visit to Gauhati and Shillong in the lower Himalayas and the centre of India's extensive tea-growing country, was cut short by China's invasion of India in 1962. For a time a significant feeling of panic prevailed. Calcutta was within bombing distance for Chinese aircraft. If this had occurred, the level of panic that would have resulted in a city the size of Calcutta doesn't bear thinking about. However, I was brought back to reality one morning, at the height of these uncertain times, when the office receptionist advised that there were two nuns who urgently wished to see me. They were from a mission high in the foothills of the Himalayas east of Gauhati. They were Australians!

Not knowing what to expect, I ventured out into the office's waiting room and there indeed were two immaculately dressed nuns resplendent in the dress of the order to which they belonged. As I crossed the floor towards them I overheard a remark of one to the other, 'Now then, doesn't he look like a very nice young man!' A good start. I settled them both into my office, offered a cup of tea and then enquired as to how I could help them. They related that as the Chinese soldiers drew nearer, the Indian authorities enforced the evacuation of all civilians in the area, including themselves. Furious at any suggestion that they should leave the mission at the mercy of foreign soldiers, whether civilians were evacuated or not, and many, including children, would remain, they demanded they be permitted to stay, arguing that another benefit/aim would be that of having the opportunity to convert some of the marauding hordes to Christianity! Of this they were very confident. The good Lord would ensure success!

One has to picture that the way out from the Mission was, by bicycle, down steep winding roads, unsurfaced, damaged by rain and truck traffic, with only a basket on the front for carrying a minimum of possessions. The demands of the authorities prevailed and off they set, ending up in Calcutta to see me two weeks later!

What did they want of me? 'Please, Mr Allgrove, help us return to the Mission!' For me, 'Mission Impossible'. Finally realising that their requests couldn't be met they embarked on a series of searching questions as to what Australia was like today, in 1962. When in response to the question, 'How long is it since you've been back to Australia?', I was taken aback when one replied, first looking at the other and then a final nod of agreement, 'Thirty years since we were in Sydney.' A then/now reply was not possible. I said, 'Wow, I wasn't born when you left Australia. Also I was born in Malaysia, went to Australia at the age of seven and first experienced Sydney, and then only the International Airport in 1949, when transiting from Adelaide to Singapore on my second visit for school holidays.'

These two incredible ladies left, and when hostilities had lapsed, returned to their 'home' at the Mission, taking with them a couple of coffee-table books containing numerous photographs of Australia of the time.

Few Europeans settled permanently in India. Life was a succession of tours, each of three to four years duration, working for one of the many companies engaged in activities such as shipping, insurance, banking, legal, tea, jute and woollen mills and, prior to independence, government, the police, public services, etc. Retirement on a good pension, and earlier than possible at home in the UK, was the general aim. Buy a small farm or orchard as my father did when retiring from Malaysia, or a home in a village away from the main cities and enjoy retirement in the very lovely English, Scottish or Welsh countryside and have the ability to visit France, Italy, Spain and Europe in general, as they were all so close and relatively cheap to get to.

In 1963 I was asked to proceed to Bombay (Mumbai today) for three months to manage Austrade's office while the incumbent Trade Commissioner, George Carr, was on leave in Australia. An opportunity not to be missed. It was suggested that rather than travel by air, the train journey from Calcutta to Bombay was a worthwhile experience.

The journey, leaving early in the evening, took about thirty-six hours, trekking north-west from Howrah Station, Calcutta, to Allahabad, and then south to Bombay. Because cuisine provided on board was suspect and minimal, most passengers travelling 'cattle class' bought from vendors at stops along the way. British agency houses, ever practical, had specially made ice boxes that fitted under the bottom bunk. These were provided to their senior executives, travelling first class, and filled with enough food, water and drink for the entire journey – cold chicken, fruit, bread and butter, beer, whisky, etc., all packed in water-proof containers surrounded by ice. One didn't have to leave one's compartment except for the necessities of nature. The reason was that one was pretty certain of escaping the ravages of 'Delhi belly'.

I was offered to avail myself of this service, which was gratefully accepted. The box was loaded onto the train and on arrival in Bombay a representative of the company boarded the train and took it away. It proved to be an incomparable service.

The two-berth cabin I occupied on my own at departure remained so until some time around two o'clock in the morning, when the train stopped. A very cultured Indian gentleman, traditionally dressed, quietly entered and crawled into the bottom bunk – I having opted for the top. Soon after dawn the train pulled into Allahabad, a substantial city, and seemingly all passengers disembarked for a stroll along the platform. I was inclined not to follow suit, as being in my pyjamas I didn't want the bother of dressing. My companion persuaded me that there was no need to dress, he wasn't going to. My first reaction, however, was one of this course of action being fine for him, because in sari and dhoti one could be forgiven for wondering whether he was in his day clothes or pyjamas. Anyway, keeping close to my fellow traveller, we ventured out onto the platform where literally hundreds, if not thousands, of individuals were milling about. Being the only white face amongst this mass of humanity was somewhat unnerving and being in conventional Western shortie pyjamas I must have looked pretty ridiculous. The close scrutiny to which I was subjected tended to confirm this. Walking the length of the train did however give me the opportunity of seeing how the majority of passengers spent their long journey. Those that could get into a carriage sat on benches randomly placed along the length of the carriage, which was an open space with a door at each end. Those that couldn't arrange themselves huddled on the roof, or even, as a last and dangerous resort, clung to the sides. The casualty rate of such a journey was never disclosed.

Goldcroft, George and Margaret Carr's apartment awaited me and much more importantly, Kuwarji, their unbelievably capable and efficient bearer. We formed a close relationship because of this. I advised Kuwarji at ten o'clock in the morning that I was having twelve guests for dinner. 'No problem, Sahib.' The telephone call was only prolonged by a request of what I should procure from the duty free shop, which would, within the hour, have all purchases delivered.

Whilst having, as with Calcutta, its slum area (if you haven't seen the film *Slumdog Millionaire*, you should), Bombay being on the coast is a much more pleasant city, and many expatriates living in Bombay had a beach cottage, often shared with others, along the coast. Through the generosity of friends, John and Bridget Hicks, I regularly had the pleasure of weekends at their cottage set under coconut palms metres from the sea. Fishermen each morning offered for sale a variety of species from their overnight trips, often having ventured a considerable distance out to sea in the darkness of night. Very relaxing, helped by the pre-lunch gin and tonics.

Being at the post in a caretaker capacity precluded becoming deeply involved with the business community – notable exceptions being those engaged in the woollen textile, engineering, milk products, shipping and banking industries.

I was privileged to meet several of those who were well within the top ten per cent of the population. Names such as Birla, Tata, Godrej, Patel, Jejeebhoy, Wadia and Mehta represented families which were the equivalents, or more so, of the Packers, Smorgans, Fairfaxs, Pratts and Murdochs of Australia. All highly educated and wealthy. A lot could be learnt from the senior personnel of the empires they presided over, particularly as to how to manage the maze of stifling bureaucracy of government and the mass of regulations that it controlled. The land of the manila folder, each tied with a red ribbon, one upon the other piled up on the desks of numerous public servants. The origin of the term 'red tape' is derived from this practice.

Sorties out of Bombay were confined to one memorable visit to the very ancient Hindu sites at Ajanta and Ellora. A must for anyone visiting southern India. A very fortunate coincidence was that I sat next to Paul Engle on the flight to Ajanta. He was a professor at Iowa State University, a Rhodes Scholar, a poet, and was very well read on matters of Indian history. The Ajanta site consists of a series of temples excavated/carved into towering cliffs along the meandering curved course of the old river, now largely dry for most of the year. Richly decorated caverns with high ceilings and endless sculptures of Indian gods and goddesses rival the tombs of the kings and queens of Egypt.

Bombay, the capital of the State of Maharashtra – an alcohol-free State – presented some problems if entertaining outside of one's home, the privacy of which permitted the serving of alcoholic drinks. One such occasion arose when a non-official Australian cricket team visited Bombay on its way to South Africa, where a series of matches were to be played in defiance of the embargo of sporting relations with what was then an apartheid practising country. Members of the team included several Australian test players (Richie Benaud and Norman O'Neill to name two), and they, and a number of accompanying journalists, all stayed at the hotel-like facilities that were part of the cricket ground. What to do? Access to Australian beer was, I was advised in advance of the team's arrival, a must! Supply was not a problem as Fosters was readily available from one of the several ships' chandlers situated in the customs-controlled area of the Port of Bombay. Their business was mainly that of supplying a wide range of goods and services to ships sailing east from Europe through the Suez Canal to the East and Australia. At that time many travelled by sea to and from the UK. Most of us can remember the P&O ships *Stratheden*, *Orcades*, *Otranto*, *Orion*, *Himalaya* and others. All today replaced by air travel, with sea journeys being confined to the cruise industry.

Entry to the ground required the flying of the Australian flag on the car, the driver in full working uniform, me in the back with my diplomatic passport, and the boot full of cases of beer. Several journeys were required! Once inside the ground, assistance was readily available, for a few rupees, to transport the precious amber liquid to two of the rooms reserved for the players. The spacious baths in these rooms were filled with ice, cases were unpacked, and my job was completed, much to the satisfaction of the team on arrival.

As colonialists, the British were masters of providing facilities to enable expatriates to relax away from the real and harsh world around them. The Bombay Gymkhama Club was one such establishment. Founded in 1875 one could find relief in enjoying the facilities provided for cricket, rugby, soccer, hockey, tennis, badminton, squash, table tennis and billiards. Regular evening entertainment was by way of Club arranged dinners and dances (often requiring black-tie as minimum dress – known as Red Sea Kit when worn without a jacket), film shows, plays and the much anticipated Rugger Review. Willing social subcommittees arranged these activities. The Club also had a shop for the convenience of members offering a wide selection of tinned provisions, household goods, linen, 'drills and twills', fresh meat, fish, vegetables and fruit. A proud boast was that Melton Mowbray Pork Pies were also available, which together with a variety of cheeses, all from the UK and Europe, made the Club very much a home away from home. Catering facilities were available for members in their homes. One cute caveat was that if the catering order exceeded fifty rupees, such crockery etc. required was supplied free of charge!

Whilst in Bombay, Mr John G. Phillips, Deputy Governor of the Reserve Bank, and his wife visited India and a memorable dinner in his honour was hosted by Shri and Shrimati P.C. Bhattacharyya, Governor of the Reserve Bank of India. Set in a large garden, party lights twinkling, some 100 plus guests and tables laden with a wide variety of dishes – an incredible buffet. It was a very special experience for me because every dish was vegetarian, not one contained meat, fish or fowl, but one wouldn't have known largely because of the clever use of soya bean products and, of course, curry condiments.

By chance I met, and became great friends with, a memorable Lady Maki D. Bhiwandiwalla. We continued to correspond for many years before her death. Maki lived very comfortably with her daughter Phiroza, they were a Parsi family. After some time Maki confided that she was widowed to a much older husband when she was barely out of her teens. It had been an arranged marriage and in his will he had insisted that his not inconsiderable wealth would only be available to her if she never remarried. Maki took little time to decide that this was fine – she wouldn't remarry, but would enjoy herself spending her inheritance. She travelled and partied at will. Not an easy choice in a very conservative society. Maki was a breath of fresh air.

There are so many more stories and experiences to be related, those involving Charles and Margaret Will, he being head of the River Stream Navigation Company, whilst Margaret worked with me in Calcutta. Margaret in particular was a pillar of strength, very British, very practical.

There was my involvement with Jigmi Diorgi, then Prime Minister of Bhutan, later assassinated in his own country. He was wishing to introduce Australian merino sheep to cross with local breeds with the aim of upgrading quality and quantity of the wool produced.

Ross and Maxine Tattam, he being area manager of Everett Steamship Company, were inseparable friends who contributed so much, so freely, to making my life so much easier in Calcutta.

Others of whom I have vivid memories include Sri Banerjee, head of Indian Railways, based in Calcutta; Mohie and Sushila Das, chairman of McKinnon McKenzie India; Samir and Sita Roy of Birla Bros (Sam and I studied together at Reading University in the UK from 1953–1956); Rex Vidler, local manager for Qantas; Ron and Shirley Rowell and Jim and Pat Lean, both Ron and Jim being seconded from GMH Melbourne to assist Hindustan Motors; Joe and Marge Lever, manager HKSB (refer to earlier story!); Cyril and Barbara Pitts, joint managing director of ICI and their daughter Katie; Servi Singh of Piggott Chapman an all India amateur squash champion, who often used me as a 'warm up' opponent before he played a major match.

On one such occasion Servi, as we approached court side, said: 'Today, John, we're playing for a case of Fosters beer.' He gave me eight points a game and service to start. Only had to win one point to clinch a set. In a three set rubber I never won a single point! This was at a time when I thought I played a reasonable game of squash.

There were many others, but I have selected those above because involving each there is a story to tell. They provide a reminder should you, the reader, and I have the pleasure of meeting in the future.

Soon after returning to Calcutta from Bombay an early morning call from Canberra enquired as to whether I minded proceeding to Athens, Greece, for 'a few months'. Mind? Athens versus Calcutta, no contest. And so my sojourn in India came to a close. The incumbent Trade Commissioner had fallen ill whilst on a short leave in the UK. Little did I realise that I was never to return to Calcutta, as after the expected period in Athens, magically being over the summer months, I was assigned to Cairo, Egypt, for the balance of my first posting overseas.

But this was not before experiencing the delights and relaxation over the weekends of the Greek islands; Corfu in summer was magic, the journey through Corinth Canal being spectacular; the Epidaurus Festival in the ancient amphitheatre at the site of the same name on the eastern shore of the Peloponnese a short romantic sail from the port of Piraeus. Acoustics of the theatre were spectacular. One could from the back row, high and distant from the stage area far below, hear a match struck. Regular pleasures experienced on many occasions, such as dinner in the numerous seafood restaurants along the foreshore of Piraeus harbour and raucous evenings in the Plaka enjoying Greek barbecues and shamelessly breaking china (supplied by the proprietors, paid for by guests), whilst singing and dancing. Journeys into the hinterland, especially Delphi, presented one with breathtaking mountainous scenery and sobering archaeological sites.

A stay that was all too short. It was interesting to realise that post-war immigration of Greeks to Australia has resulted in Melbourne having the second largest Greek community of any city in the world. Only second to Athens, and now perhaps Salonika.

How fortuitous this would turn out to be. It was in Cairo that I met Maureen, later to become my lover, wife and long-time friend from late 1963 until the present day. We were married in Sydney on 24 January 1966.

CHAPTER TWO

Cairo, Egypt

1963–1964

Post included responsibilities for Australia's trade interests in Egypt, Sudan, Libya, West Coast of Saudi Arabia and Yemen.

A short flight from Athens to Cairo in mid 1963 where I was met by Frank Atkins, who not only was to be my boss, but together with his wife Barbara and their family, to become my life-long friends. Frank had fought as a member of the AIF in North Africa during World War Two and had a great understanding of the Egyptian people (a complex mix), and of North Africa itself. The drive with Frank from Cairo to Benghazi via Alexandria, through the battlefields of El Alamein, Mersa Matruh, crossing the border into Libya just before Bardia, and thence to Tobruk, Derna, and finally to Benghazi itself, was a fascinating experience. Sealed road the whole way, desert as far as the eye could see.

The annual rainfall is so low throughout the region that the preservation of anything left on the ground (or buried e.g. the tombs of the Egyptian kings), was largely spared deterioration. Just off the road (this is 1963–1964, just twenty years after the height of the conflicts of World War Two), we found gas masks, grenades, tyres, pieces of destroyed tanks and on ridges, if one dug into the sand, many spent rifle and machine gun bullets. Obviously there had been much more, but the desert Arabs, the Bedouin, had seen to the disappearance of anything of value long before.

During the relatively short period spent in Libya (two to three visits), I was fortunate to visit Leptis Magna and the ancient Greek/Roman ruins outside Benghazi. Only a personal visit will satisfy those interested in the marvels erected during these civilisations. All a memorable history lesson.

My first day in the office was interesting. My predecessor, one Jim Scully, later to become Secretary of the Department of Trade, had spread the rumour amongst the female members of the Embassy, that his replacement was a sex maniac! On moving into the secure section of the Embassy to meet staff I found they were all in the office safe peeping out occasionally to see what this new colleague looked like. The lie was soon revealed. Included in that moment was when I first met Maureen.

A great photograph of Maureen on a camel at the pyramids is often presented by me as being that of my first vision of the girl I was to marry. Not so, but it doesn't really matter.

At the apex of the fertile Nile Delta that spreads to the port of Alexandria to the north-west and Port Said to the north-east, Cairo is situated on the banks of the Nile, which is fed by flows from Uganda far to the south, through Sudan (White Nile), joining with the Blue Nile at Khartoum, to become the mighty River Nile flowing through Egypt, in all over 4000 miles (6500 kilometres).

A fascinating city in itself, the Cairo Museum houses the treasures from the tomb of King Tutankhamun and others. The stately feluccas sailing on the Nile, and the markets – Cairo is the starting point for so much more.

On the edge of the Delta, just outside Cairo are the famous Pyramids of Giza, the largest being Cheops. The Sphinx is situated in the same area with the step pyramid of Saqqara to the south.

The landscape is dramatic as one moves in a step from the green rice fields and date-palmed Delta to the desert stretching endlessly to the west as far as one can see – nothing, just sand.

One then moves south to Karnak where the Temple of Amun (Great Hall of Pillars of King Sethos I and Ramesses II), is situated. At Thebes lies the incredible Temple of Queen Hatshepsut carved into the cliffs which tower above. Here also the Memnon Colossi. These are two huge statues of seated figures being the only remains of the funerary temple of King Amenophis III. The tomb of the better-known Queen Nefertiti one finds here also.

On to Luxor for the temple of Amun-Mut-Khonsu and others and the Great Court of King Ramesses III. In the Valley of the Kings was found intact the tomb of Tutankhamen, intact being the operative word. Much smaller than tombs of other kings, its finding unearthed unbelievable treasures. One can hardly imagine the scale and grandeur of the treasures long since looted from the larger tombs. Onwards and onwards south to Abu Simbel to view the colossal statues of King Ramesses and the rock temples.

Aswan Dam was being built with Russian aid during my time in Egypt. President Khrushchev visited to breach the diversion dam, necessary during construction of the main dam to allow the waters of the Nile to flow through the large pipes feeding the turbines of the massive hydropower station already largely completed. Great idea and the time had come, but someone forgot to tell a number of workers having their lunch whilst seated in one of these pipes! Made pretty interesting reading in the next day's press – 'Workers Washed Down the Nile' etc. On another occasion a huge truck carrying cement from the batching plant on the banks of the Nile was filled just at knock-off time for the shift then operating. Unfortunately it happened to be the last shift of the day! It was found next morning with its load of cement slurry very, very much set! Again eyewitness accounts of men with jack hammers at work, yes, you get the picture, made hilarious viewing.

I want to avoid this becoming a history lesson by very much an amateur, but let some of these comments encourage you, as the reader, to visit this very special and spectacular spot in the world.

Suffice to conclude by saying that Egyptian chronology is based on the rules of their Kings (Pharaohs). Its history covers thirty-three dynasties from the foundation of the State until the last native king before Alexander the Great, a period from 3000 BC.

The work day regime in Cairo was different from that experienced before. Office hours began at 7 am and concluded at 2 pm. After what was a late lunch, one was free to have a rest, the preferred activity of the local population, or a round of golf and then a short sleep or visit to the markets, my preferred activity, before going out in the evening to one of the endless social functions, business or purely pleasure. At around 5 pm, government officials and businesses reopened for a couple of hours. To meet the required number of hours per week for Embassy staff, Thursday was the long day of the week, 7 am through to 7.30 pm.

One memorable social function took place at a formal dinner given by Frank and Barbara. After a lengthy period of pre-dinner drinks guests were seated and entree served by Mohamed and his helper, gliding almost invisibly around the table. Main course was a full and elaborately decorated ham to be carved by Frank, vegetables to be served by staff. As Mohamed entered the room he slipped and the ham left the plate and not so slowly slid across the floor until contact with the wall brought it to an abrupt stop. No one said a word, all having their own thoughts as to what would happen next! Frank poured another drink, Mohamed, quite undeterred, picked up the ham and returned it to the kitchen. We all waited.

It was quite some time before Mohamed returned, smiling, almost a triumphant look on his face, bearing, on the same plate, a large roast turkey.

Dinner continued with many theories as to how 'the miracle' was achieved. Next morning Barbara was stepping from the lift at ground level when the wife of the Reuter's correspondent to the region living in Cairo, well known to us, happened to emerge from the adjoining block. Greetings were exchanged following which Barbara's neighbour said, 'Barbara, strange thing happened last night, we had guests to dinner and I'm sure I had asked our cook to prepare a roast turkey, but instead a large ham appeared.' Barbara laughed. The truth was out. Mohamed, ever-resourceful, had dashed next door (two lift journeys of several floors), and made the swap. Both sets of guests were blissfully unaware, but well satisfied.

Not common for food exchanges, but staff borrowing serving dishes, flower vases, extra cutlery and crockery from a neighbour without their respective employers knowing was common and an accepted practice. On more than one occasion I attended a dinner party and recognised something from my own kitchen!

The dry warm weather for many months of the year enabled frequent outdoor outings for families. Picnics along the Suez Canal – ships passing through being almost touchable – were popular for Maureen and I and our friends, particularly Ray and Lyn Jeppesen. Ray was Qantas manager for North Africa.

Excursions into the desert, perhaps visiting the War Grave Cemeteries at El Alamein had great historical interest and relevance for Australians.

A very significant trade success for the Australian arm of an American company, Le Tourneau Westinghouse, occurred when they secured a large order for earthmoving equipment, purchased by Egyptian Desert Reclamation Organisation, that was undertaking large scale rehabilitation work in desert regions between the Nile and Red Sea. At the time it was the most significant export order ever awarded to an Australian-based manufacturer of capital goods.

After the six-day war between Egypt and Israel, just a short time later, Le Tourneau received a sizeable order for spares for this equipment – ordered against the provision of part and serial numbers. That was clear and understood, but the order came from Israel! Yes, all the equipment purchased and paid for by Egypt had been captured during the war.

The understanding of cultural customs I found to be more important in Arab countries than those of the Far East, where good manners were, as a beginning, sufficient to develop a relationship of trust.

There is a clear distinction between developing a relationship, and that of developing trust between two parties. The latter, together with understanding some dos and don'ts, is of paramount importance before the closure and successful realisation of any business deal. A signed contract is not worth the paper it's written on if trust doesn't exist. In the event of a dispute, satisfactory settlement is often very difficult and usually a lengthy, costly process. Arbitration will be according to the laws and procedures of the 'local regime'. Many Westerners believe that all they have to achieve is a signature on a contract. So much can occur between that event and subsequent delivery of an export order. There must be trust.

Also, among the dos and don'ts are those the average Australian businessmen would not necessarily think of. Always accept coffee that will be offered at the beginning of a meeting. Don't drink it if you don't want to, but never refuse the offer. Preferably of course one should drink the strong coffee that is customarily served, the result being that at the end of a day of appointments, I found I was pretty high on caffeine! Other customs to be aware of included never, when seated, crossing one's legs so the sole of the shoe faced the other party. Equally important was never to show the palm of your hand directly to anyone. Both regarded as very rude.

A number of experiences when dealing with businessmen in countries to which I travelled from Cairo are of interest. One involved Sheik Awadi, the CEO of the Arab Trading company in Jeddah, Saudi Arabia. Sales of wheat flour, live sheep, dairy products and a wide range of processed items found on supermarket shelves, were of great interest to potential Australian suppliers, particularly that of wheat flour by the Australian Wheat Board (AWB). After some months and several visits I felt that a visit to Australia, under the provisions of the Special Projects Visits Fund, by Sheik Awadi, would materially assist in securing a multi-million dollar contract. Tickets for the Sheik and one or two members of his staff were offered, with initial discussions as to when the visit should take place, together with those other details that make up the planning of a VIP visit. I was stopped in my tracks when, whilst seemingly being interested in such a visit, Sheik

Awadi, with I detected was a slight smile, said that tickets would not be necessary as he would travel in his own aircraft, accompanied by a not insignificant number of his wives.

Attitudes in Canberra, and indeed most of our hotels, were certainly not as liberal in 1963 as now. Canberra got cold feet and the visit never took place, replaced by further visits to Saudi Arabia by AWB personnel and specialist technicians from the Australian Bread Institute. The Saudis had to be convinced that Australian flour made from high protein wheat, was as good, or better, than flour from the USA for making their customary flat unleavened bread.

Sudan, a country serviced from Cairo, meant visiting Khartoum about twice a year. Prospects for the development of meaningful trade, except for grains and supermarket goods, minimal. However, even in my short exposure to this now divided nation, a couple of experiences stand out and are worth relating.

Arriving in Khartoum by air from Cairo for my first visit, I checked into the hotel, took a walk in the surrounding palm dominated gardens, which extended to the banks of the River Nile, and wondered at the sight of the still but flowing waters, before venturing into the bar for a pre-lunch gin and tonic. Outside it was forty degrees plus! It was a Sunday.

Only one other person, perched on a bar stool, was present. In flowing white robes in stark contract to his jet black skin, a mountain of a man with a flashing smile, he invited me to join him, which I did without hesitation. There was an educated look about Ibrahim El Nawal, a descendent of the Mhadi. He was a cotton broker.

A light lunch together and then we were off to Omdurman, situated virtually as a suburb of Khartoum. Once away from the banks of the Nile one soon enters a landscape that is pure desert to the horizon. Ibrahim first took me to the camel market, advising me to stay close to him and not make any gestures that may cause offence.

The market doubled as a trading area for camels and the firewood and carpets that their owners had brought with them on the long journey from the south. In exchange they took back salt, flour, sugar and other life necessities. All this was done on foot, the load on the way back borne by a few camels and human bearers.

From my perspective, given the background against which I had grown up, I must say that I had then, and to this day, never witnessed such an evil-looking group of human beings. The look in those dark eyes eyeing one below large bushy eyebrows above an impressive moustache and black beard. I needed no encouragement in ensuring I stayed very close to Ibrahim!

We then drove towards the site of the famous Battle of Omdurman passing a camel train on its way to the market. The otherwise flat flint-stoned landscape, where the conflict occurred, had just one large mound, taking about half an hour to climb while Ibrahim waited in his car at the base. It was from here that the Mahdi and his thousands of troops in 1898 awaited the arrival, from boats on the Nile, of Lord Kitchener on his quest to conquer the Sudan for the British crown. Kitchener's troops with more modern arms, including machine-guns, prevailed over Abdullah al Tashi, the Mahdi, with some 9000 Mahdists dying in the process. Kitchener was driven by a desire to avenge the death of General Gordon in Khartoum some time before.

The battle had been waged some sixty-five years prior to my visit in 1963, but an eeriness was evident. Interestingly, close to the site is an obelisk-type monument to a number of New Zealanders, who fought and died as members of Kitchener's troops.

Several photographs later we returned to the outskirts of Khartoum, Ibrahim having invited me to his home for an early dinner. It was an impressive establishment of several floors behind a walled compound. Women's quarters were hidden by ornately carved screens, through which numerous pairs of eyes could be seen to one side. Men's quarters were to the other side. Coffee was presented being prepared by first roasting green beans, grinding and finally infused and filtered through fibres from the trunk of banana palms. Delicious. Whilst absorbing all around me and marvelling at the instantaneous trust that had been developed between us, the call to prayers from the nearby mosque was heard loud and clear. This came from the top of the tall tower dominating the skyline above a moderate dome.

When I commented that the mullah making the call must get sick of ascending the numerous steps to the top several times a day, Ibrahim took me over to a room at the tower's base. There lay the mullah on a hessian bed next to a player. All he had to do was raise an arm and place the needle on the record. Very advanced technology for that part of the world in 1963.

To keep my appointment with the manager of a department store I arrived soon after nine in the morning. Upon enquiring as to the location of his office I was shown to the rear of the establishment, across a small garden and to a free-standing 'shed'. On entering I found four to five men around a table, that of the manager, which was covered with empty bottles of beer! I discovered they had been drinking most of the night! After introductions, the question that required an answer was: 'Why?'

Several of those gathered were airline staff, including a pilot, of Saudi Arabian Airways, which was then staffed by TWA personnel from the USA, for flight deck and engineering crew. The previous afternoon those gathered were all taking a flight from Jeddah to Riyadh, the capital of Saudi Arabia, when midway the captain received a call that they should return to Jeddah to pick up some live sheep, which were required by one of the sheiks of the royal family for a feast that evening. Orders to be obeyed, the flight turned, picked up the sheep and the original flight recommenced. Problem? Because of the delay some passengers became hungry. A sheep was slaughtered, a fire lit on a sheet of iron and the roasting began at 25,000 feet, all the time without the knowledge of the flight deck. On opening the door into the cabin area, the captain was met with clouds of smoke and the aroma of roasting lamb. Undeterred he shut the door, landed at Riyadh and later piloted the same plane on its scheduled, but delayed, flight to Khartoum. Still visibly shaken and unable to sleep, the crew descended on the store manager, whom they knew well and so began the nerve-calming drinking session. When I arrived I was invited to join in. C'mon, at 9 am? But there was more to come. Before settling into the manager's office, all involved had set out from Khartoum for a desert barbecue to a site near where the famous Battle of Omdurman was waged some 165 years earlier. No sooner had the fire been lit than shells, fired during an army exercise, started whistling overhead. Fortunately they were under an overhanging cliff as any shell falling short could certainly have proved fatal. A hasty retreat to the manager's office, by now near midnight, and the shattered nerves from the day's events were anaesthetised by alcohol. Needless to say I declined the offer to stay and returned out into the over forty degree heat of Khartoum.

In light of subsequent events I am pleased I visited the Sudan when I did.

During my Cairo posting I visited the Yemen twice only: Aden, situated at the very south of the Arabian Peninsula with Saudi Arabia to the north; and Bahrain, Qatar, the United Arab Emirates (Dubai) and Oman to the north-east and east. A bustling and strategic port facing the Gulf of Aden and the entrance to the Red Sea.

Of great significance to me, because it was here that I purchased the black pearl that was to be the centre of the self-designed engagement ring that I hoped Maureen would accept when I returned to Australia in late December 1964, she having concluded her posting and returned to Australia in mid year.

Being aware that such natural pearls could be found in Aden I was taken through a labyrinth of alleys to a dealer who crouched over a counter displaying his wares, one by one, on a velvet cloth. In full Arab dress and wearing dark glasses the encounter was somewhat off-putting as I couldn't meet his gaze. Suffice to say, unfairly maybe, that the atmosphere was confronting and a little evil!

A choice was made, a deal done and I happily departed ready to do business with a jeweller in Cairo. The design was simple; twelve small diamonds surrounding a central solitary pearl in a silver setting. It turned out just as I had imagined and, most importantly, Maureen was delighted when she said, 'Yes.'

A sad sequel however was to follow as the pin setting which secured the pearl proved unreliable and whilst in Seoul years later, the pearl was lost. Replacement with a normal white pearl took place whilst stationed there, but never to be forgotten was the effort and satisfaction that followed the purchase of the black pearl and the production of the original ring.

An interesting city Aden in that it is divided into three parts each being in an extinct volcano, each joined together by a tunnel linking the three craters. Virtually no vegetation and fiercely hot in summer.

Neither time nor necessity permitted journeying into the hinterland of this fascinating part of the world. But one could but marvel at the contrast between those living an unchanged life from those in biblical times, and those that occupied grand palaces, often built for strategic/security reasons, on mountain tops.

Many an untold tale remains:

- Barbecues in the desert west of the pyramid's location being reached on horseback
- Losing (then finding, thankfully), the car keys whilst swimming in the Red Sea well south of Suez
- Anxious moments after my then boss's son was bitten by a scorpion in the desert between Cairo and Alexandria. The question was whether the scorpion was green or black? If black, it could have been fatal.
- The night I ran over a dog on my way home from an evening out with Maureen. Surrounded by an angry mob, which thought I had run over a man and compensation was sought. Only saved by an English-speaking Egyptian who told me to walk away slowly, don't look around, drive off and he would do the rest.
- The hot bellybutton of an exotic belly dancer pressed into my

face when I suddenly turned around from the dinner table whilst attending a function late in the evening at a Cairo nightclub. These, and others, I'll leave for another occasion.

And so ended my first posting overseas, split between periods in Calcutta, Bombay, Athens and Cairo.

We spent 1965 in Canberra, Maureen switching jobs from one in the Department of Foreign Affairs to that of Secretary to the Deputy Secretary of the Department of Trade. During the year I was tasked with preparing a guide to foreign investment in a number of South-East Asian countries, which was published internally.

When advised that my next posting was to be Hong Kong, thoughts turned to an expected exciting assignment, which followed a few days after Maureen and I were married in Sydney on 24 January 1966. There was no honeymoon, we arriving in Hong Kong, after a few days in Perth, early in February.

CHAPTER THREE

Hong Kong, Hong Kong

1966–1967

Flying into Kai Tak Airport at the beginning of a new posting was an experience in itself. Approaching from the west we descended between high-rise apartment buildings, able to see families at their dinner tables. A little too close for comfort.

The office overlooked Victoria Harbour, a 24/7 hive of activity with junk, barges and ferries criss-crossing the dark waters in an endless seemingly chaotic fashion. Many ships anchored in the harbour, discharging and loading into junks which then transported their cargoes to shore. So distracting was this view, that I had to turn my desk around so that my back was to it!

This was Hong Kong thirty-one years before being handed back to the Peoples Republic of China (PRC) at the conclusion of the treaty between Britain and China some six decades earlier. British sovereignty officially transferred to China at midnight on 30 June 1997, beginning the implementation of a 'one country, two systems' arrangement. A British administration presided over by the Governor. Hong Kong, a duty-free port for all but a handful of items, was an efficient, law-abiding colony that provided an entry point into mainland China and Macau, especially for financial settlements for goods and services shipped directly to China via entry ports such as Shanghai, Hangzhou, Dalian and others.

Hong Kong proved a refreshing environment in which to work. A close relationship was developed between Philip Searcy, the Senior Trade Commissioner – and equally so between his wife Elizabeth and Maureen. Elizabeth became godmother to our firstborn, David.

A British administration made dealing with various departments easy to understand. A high degree of honesty, minimal bribery (compare the Middle East experience) and very few restrictions to trade, meant that one could concentrate on meaningfully seeking opportunities for Australian exporters and assist those that were already in the market when required. Being a tourist's paradise, taking advantage of the duty free availability of a wide spectrum of retail goods meant we experienced a constant stream of visitors, many of whom were fortunate to have Maureen as a guide.

The activities of the post included a series of market promotions for fresh and processed food products. The annual oranges, apples and pears promotions were major events involving the Miss Australia of the year. The Sunkist brand of citrus fruit from California provided the main competition, and Australian producers suffered from their inability to market under one brand as effectively practised by Californian growers. The same sorry story that exists today, with interstate rivalry between South Australia and Victoria. Now, many years later, solving the problem of the distribution of the waters of the Murray River faces the same obstacles, compounded by the competing needs of meeting scientific realities and social consequences. A big political problem results. One day whilst visiting Macau I came across a small Chinese rural worker, squatting on the foreshore, with a basket of Chinese oranges on one side and an empty basket on the other. Between the two he sat with a purple inkpad and stamp, the latter read 'Sunkist'. One by one oranges were transferred from one basket to the other, gaining the 'Sunkist' stamp on the way. Loaded onto a junk they then set sail for Hong Kong to be sold as Californian oranges such was the popularity of the brand. Equal quality? That was something else.

The beginnings of what is now a very active and significant Australian Chamber of Commerce began with meetings being held in the Trade Commissioner's office during my assignment in Hong Kong. It was seen as being desirable as the spectrum of Australian businesses seeking to become established in Hong Kong broadened. Whilst a high level of English being spoken by the Chinese business community made communications relatively easy, this did not obviate the necessity to understand the vital importance of the development of relationships if one is to succeed in doing business in Hong Kong. True anywhere, yes, but in Hong Kong with a veneer provided by a British colonial administration, one often missed the effort required to understand, and penetrate, the cultural divide. This became more and more important as the service industries were increasingly targeted by Australian companies, such as banking, insurance, architectural, accounting and legal. The Chamber has provided a fertile vehicle for the sharing of experiences, of the exchange of information that in many cases has resulted in the saving of much time and possibly anguish.

This was our first year of marriage and living in an environment that worked, and from a 'doing business' perspective that was relatively straightforward and uncomplicated, meant that our personal life was free to develop unhindered. There was golf, tennis, swimming and lunch or dinner functions on a junk on the living waters of the harbour or on the other side of the island on one of the floating restaurants in Aberdeen Harbour, as well as numerous visits to one of the many islands close by, often to attend a local festival such as the Bun Festival on Lantau or visiting the already mentioned Macau for a flutter or two at the dog track, one of Stanley Ho's many gambling venues. On balance we usually came out about even on the day!

David Anthony, our firstborn, arrived on 4 April 1967 at the Matilda Hospital situated on the peak on Hong Kong Island. Maureen spent about a week in hospital, normal in those days. Each afternoon I received a call from one of the nurses enquiring as to whether I would be joining Maureen for dinner. Answer was always in the affirmative and after arriving at around 6 pm we'd sit together on the balcony of Maureen's room, have a cocktail, then dinner, all in an idyllic setting overlooking the sea and myriad islands with China in the background.

Also 'Knutsford of Millbrook' joined the family. A large tan and white male Boxer, which we inherited from Philip's predecessor, Ted

Jarvis. The story of this acquisition is a long tale in itself, but one which ultimately gave us endless pleasure.

The Cultural Revolution was gathering momentum on the mainland, soon to have an impact on Hong Kong, where the Red Guards had their supporters. People took to the streets waving their little red books, the writings of Mao Tse Tung, and shouting anti-Western slogans. Intimidating as these demonstrations were, they never really became ugly and, probably under instructions from Beijing, soon calmed down, but not before Maureen, on her way to the office to meet me for lunch one day, became caught in the middle of the shouting masses. Carried along by the crowd was a frightening experience until a shop doorway provided a quick exit. Safe but late for lunch!

Philip's previous assignment had been in Tokyo, where he and Elizabeth befriended the then West German Ambassador and his wife. On their way home on leave the six of us dined out at an upmarket Chinese restaurant, one dish being lobster sashimi (raw lobster). The whole lobster was presented on a large flat dish with its back shell removed revealing the translucent flesh. Lobsters have a very simple nervous system resulting in a skilled chef being able to slice the body of meat into pieces, easily removed with chopsticks, without hurting the lobster itself. All well and good, providing one doesn't touch a nerve. So there was the whole crustacean laid out with its eyes and feelers moving in front of us all. Demonstrating to their guests as to how one tackles this dish, Elizabeth inserted her chopsticks and, yes, you've guessed it, touched a nerve leading to one of the legs, where upon the lobster started walking off the plate! As its claws caught the tablecloth it accelerated. At this point Mrs German Ambassador fainted, falling to the floor much to the embarrassment of us all, including the restaurant's waiters. Needless to say, one agitated lobster was removed, being replaced by the next, this time cooked, treasure from the sea.

Hong Kong was a significant importer of Australian leather, which was re-exported to mainland China where it was used in the manufacture of shoes and sandals for the lower end of the market against contracts from the larger retailers in Australia: Myer, David Jones, and stores such as Target and Big W of today. I came to know well a Chinese trader, who facilitated this trade, both ways, out of Hong Kong. He had travelled to visit his principals on several occasions, Melbourne and Adelaide being his main destinations, but never overland between the two.

He warmed to my suggestion that on his next visit he should go by car from Melbourne to Adelaide. Arrangements were made and dates set. However, departure from Melbourne was delayed on the given day, requiring an overnight stay in Keith, a more different environment one cannot imagine compared with Hong Kong. The story is now taken up as relayed to me on his return to Hong Kong. 'John, we arrived at the hotel in Keith and I was shown to my room upstairs. It was late in the evening, I switched on the light and there it was hanging, just the globe, no shade, from the middle of the ceiling. Bed, table, chair, cupboard, old curtains and something like a toilet behind the cupboard. What was this, I thought? Later I discovered it was, what you say? Yes, a bidet! After dinner with my hosts, I went to bed, but not before putting my shoes outside the door to be cleaned. The bathroom (shower, toilet etc.), was along the passage. Getting into bed I realised that I had to get up to turn out the light, the switch being by the door. Next morning I found my shoes just where I'd left them. Seeing a young lady (maid) in the passage, I politely enquired as to why my shoes hadn't been polished. Her reply was abrupt and immediate: "You shouldn't worry, mate, you're bloody lucky they're still here." With that she walked away, never to be seen again. Bit different from the Hyatt or Hilton in Hong Kong!' History doesn't relate, but I doubt very much whether the said journey was ever again undertaken by car.

Our stay in Hong Kong was cut short by about a year when a call from Sir Alan Westerman, Secretary of the Department of Trade, advised that he would like me to open a new post in Taipei, Republic of China (Taiwan). A great challenge awaited us both. We arrived after briefing back in Canberra, in September 1967.

CHAPTER FOUR

Taipei, Taiwan

1967–1969

An essential prerequisite was to understand the history of Taiwan, at least since 1895 when China ceded the island of Formosa to Japan in perpetuity. China had settled Formosa in the 17th century, making it a province in 1887.

Under the Cairo Declaration of 1943, the UK and USA pledged to restore the island of Formosa to China. What followed was a betrayal of a trusting people.

After the end of the World War Two in 1945, the Formosans, despite the Cairo Declaration, hoped for a guaranteed neutrality under American or international trusteeship. Under the Japanese, law and order was brought to the country, its people were educated and resources developed, but after the Japanese surrender in 1945, Formosans were delivered over to another and more oppressive occupation in the form of hordes of often brutal, ignorant and greedy Chinese from the mainland escaping the Mao Tse Tung Communist takeover. These were the days of the Nationalist Army spearheaded by General Chiang Kai-shek and his son Chiang Ching-kuo.

The situation reached boiling point in February 1947, when Formosans rose en masse to demand reforms. Though unarmed, Chiang Kai-shek's answer was a brutal massacre when thousands died, including the islands leaders who had asked for American help. Their pleas were ignored. Taiwan became the intended launching pad for the recovery of the mainland and the restoration of the Republic of China headquartered in Beijing (Peking).

On arriving in Taipei in September 1967, accompanied by Maureen and our then eighteen-month-old son, David, we had to start from scratch, find somewhere to live, establish an office and be ready to service the needs of Australian businessmen and government officers involved in trade matters from day one. On the domestic front, especially having a young child, this was greatly helped by having access to the American Post Exchange (PX), a benefit accorded to those holding a diplomatic passport.

Furnishing the house we found in Tienmu was an unexpected challenge. Western-style requirements could not be met 'off-the-shelf', so we resorted to pictures from magazines of dining room table and chairs, lounge-room sets, bedroom arrangements (beds, cupboards etc), indeed all that was basically made from wood and appropriate for the needs of a Western family. These we took along to one or more of many skilled craftsmen who copied from the photos to perfection. For example, eight dining chairs, plus two carvers, each made by hand with no discernible difference detectable between the eight chairs when completed.

A time-consuming, though rewarding, exercise. Great disappointment, however, when all was disposed of when the Embassy closed following the federal elections of 1972.

As the Chinese from the mainland controlled the government, the armed forces, local government, education and health services ensured that those from the mainland had preferential treatment in all aspects of life. There were, however, a number of very significant successful businesses owned and operated by Taiwanese, which had grown and prospered under Japanese occupation. A measure of the distrust and indeed hate that these Taiwanese businessmen or women had of 'mainlanders', was demonstrated by the fact that no locally engaged employee of the Australian Commissioner's office accompanying a visiting Australian businessman to that Taiwanese company, would be permitted entry, unless they too were Taiwanese. This meant that on my staff I had to have at least one marketing officer that met this required criteria. Advertising for such a prospective employee was immediately met with cries of discrimination from those who had themselves benefited from a discriminatory education! However, I persisted, and from countless applications selected an excellent individual. Before confirming his appointment I called in the rest of the staff already engaged, some five or six in all, and all of mainland origin, and asked them to spend a whole day with Donald Hung, at the end of which they re-assembled to answer a simple question, 'Are you all prepared to have Donald as one of your colleagues?' A unanimous, 'Yes, with great pleasure', was their response and so, as the first Australian Trade Commissioner's office in Taipei, we were all set to roll.

During these uncertain times, Chiang Kai-shek kept telling 'his people' that it would not be long before he would lead the invasion of the Chinese mainland, overthrow the Communist regime (PRC) and reinstate the legitimate government of the Chinese people, the Republic of China (ROC). This vow was reiterated every 10 October, the day that both the ROC and PRC celebrate as China's National Day – about the only thing that both agree on! The net result was slow economic development, especially in government-funded infrastructure. On the other hand private sector investment, especially by American firms in the electronic orientated industries, was progressing rapidly with the easily trainable and readily available labour. Many a young girl came out of the paddy fields and joined others labouring on an assembly line. The production of television sets, washing machines, dryers, dishwashers etc. for world markets gathered momentum. Rice cookers, made by companies such as Taitung, rolled off the assembly lines for Asian markets.

An interesting reality was that during the night fishing boats would leave the western seaboard of Taiwan and venture to the middle of the China Sea. There they would meet similar vessels from mainland China and exchange goods that each other's population wanted, swapping modern appliances for items such as Chinese medicines. All of this not withstanding that each country was technically at war with each other.

Australia's trade interests were not extensive – wool, wool-waste products, dairy products, wheat and barley, consumer products, mainly processed foods and beverages sold through the PX and a limited, but growing, number of retail outlets.

Politically Australia's reason for having an Embassy in Taipei at all was the expectation that this would provide an authoritative source of information of developments on the mainland. This did not eventuate to any marked degree due, I believe in part, to the disinterest of appointed staff. Inevitably Australia would change its recognition of the ROC to that of the PRC, as had many other countries, including one of the first to do so, the United Kingdom. Australia followed suit immediately after the Whitlam Labor government won office in 1972. When this occurred, the Australian embassy in Taipei was closed.

However, the Trade Commissioner's office had formed a very close relationship with both the public and private sector at the most senior levels. I am often asked which posting I enjoyed the most. From a professional viewpoint, Taipei remains my response. Our daughter, Anne-Marie, was born in Taipei on a cold winter's night in February 1969, this magical event providing material for an amusing story.

Arriving home from the office on the day of Anne-Marie's entry into the world, I found Maureen suggesting that she felt today was to be the day. The bag was packed, we settled down for dinner, plus a glass or two of wine. Maureen then put on her nightdress and gown and at a certain point around 10 pm she said, 'OK darling, let's go!'

It happened to be Chinese New Year and everyone was on holiday, and this included all but a skeleton staff at the Seventh Day Adventists Hospital to which we were headed.

Behind the hallway situated admissions counter sat an aged Chinese lady, who indicated that the lift wasn't functioning and a walk up three flights of stairs confronted Maureen. With courage and difficulty she managed, I bringing her bag up later, and the one nurse in attendance ushered us BOTH into a 'holding pen' containing curtained cubicles,

Maureen being directed to one and ME to one adjoining! Maureen was invited to lie down on her hard, raised platform of a bed. Then a shrill voice uttered in very broken English, 'And you mister, you lie down too!' Too shocked, even bordering on terror, I obeyed, my eyes then being drawn to the images around the edge of the ceiling. Full-size paintings, in colour, of the events leading to the birth of a child. Conception, coming together of ovum and sperm, monthly growth of the foetus in the womb and finally arrival into the world! Beautiful, but 'ugh'!

Time between contractions lessened and soon it was into the delivery room. It took some effort to persuade the sole nurse in attendance (who I might add was weather-beaten and looked as though she may have swum across the Yangzte with Mao Tse Tung and delivered thousands of babies) that I would be present, as I have with three of our four children, at the birth.

Resigned to my insistence, I was ushered to another room, told to remove all clothing, save underpants, and put on theatre garments, a bundle being handed to me. Well, what a sight! Cut to fit a short Chinese figure, the trousers of these white cotton garments reached to just below my knees, the sailor jacket-like top had billowing sleeves to the elbows and the cotton socks, well they were pretty much like those used in the theatre of a Western hospital. Of the same material a 'shower cap' was placed on my head.

When I walked into the delivery room accompanied by the one young house doctor on duty, Maureen was already in labour. She looked at me, burst out laughing to which I responded by insisting she concentrate on what she was doing. How very fortunate we were, she in particular. What followed was a perfectly natural birth, no instruments required. With that I asked Maureen if there was anything she would like. 'A gin tonic' was her reply – all this at 2 am!

I was required to wheel her to her as-yet-unseen room, past the glass-walled nursery, which incidentally was the one reasonably immaculate part of the whole hospital. On entering we were presented with an unbelievable sight. The room had not been touched since the previous occupant had vacated. Dirty, stained sheets, waste-paper baskets full of tissues etc. No use complaining as there was no one to do anything! Making Maureen comfortable in a lounge chair, I ventured forth into the cold wet still dark morning to fetch from home all requirements – clean linen, towels, soap, toilet paper, blankets – everything your mind can imagine. On my return I cleaned the room without there being any hot water – 'Chinese New Year, boiler turned off!', was the explanation provided. Anyway, Maureen's doctor, one Dr Dale, a red-haired Canadian Seventh Day Adventist returned around dawn, whereupon I gave him a not to be disputed ultimatum, that I would be taking mother and child home forthwith – Maureen having only spent a few hours in bed. With the comforts and facilities at home, including the help of Maureen's mother who had come up from Sydney for the big event, we would manage. This we did, and so began Anne-Marie's life in this big wide wonderful world!

Business experiences, some very different from those one would expect at home, were many. One involved a protracted difference of opinion that I had with the Australian Dairy Board regarding the branding of Australian butter that was to be shipped to Taiwan in bulk and packaged into retail packs. The Board wished, in fact insisted, that graphics on packaging be the same as those used in a number of other markets – 'Kangaroo' Brand Butter with the obvious logo. I advised that the opinion of their Taiwanese 'partners' should be listened to very carefully, they politely pointing out that the Chinese character for rat was almost the same as that for kangaroo. With due respect to the ADPB, they felt that supermarket, or corner store, shoppers would be disinclined to buy 'rat' butter, even if the graphic portrayed a kangaroo.

Soon, very soon, after arriving in Taipei, an Australian Trade Mission managed by a departmental official (not to be named even though now deceased), set foot in Taiwan, probably the first ever.

Individual businessmen yes; but an official government-sponsored mission this was the first.

Hospitality protocols called for one major dinner hosted by the Australian visitors, another some one or two days apart, by the hosts. After the latter many from both groups moved on to the Queen Bee in Taipei's entertainment district. Establishments of this kind, of which there were several, had never been seen by mission members before. Spread over several floors, each having many rooms, much like a hotel, but without individual en suites, nominal furniture and one or two low tables. Six or so men entered a room, soon to be followed by a similar number of generally lovely young Taiwanese maidens. Drinks flowed and much chatting and laughter, although somewhat limited by the language barrier. Soon everyone was paired off! That was it. Though cost for the next hour or so was not disclosed, it would not have come cheaply. As events came to a close, the music ceased, Mama-San entered and immediately noticed the Mission's esteemed manager obviously finding his 'partner' of great interest. She asked if I thought he would like to take her home, back to the hotel. My response was, 'Of course, look at him, no need to ask!' Members of the mission went back to the hotel, and I returned home.

Next morning I arrived, only to be met on entering the lounge set aside for the daily briefing with howls of laughter. An explanation as to the cause of all the hilarity followed. Said manager, plus partner, had entered his room and closed the door. Undressing, at least to underwear – let's call him Charlie – Charlie lay on the bed and waited, expectantly! Young lass had gone into the bathroom to have a shower, lots of warm water, soap, clean fluffy towels – what luxury, but didn't reappear. Impatience got the better of Charlie who tentatively opened the bathroom door and what he saw killed any desires or fantasies he may have had.

Said damsel was sitting, stark naked, on the side of the bath busily cleaning, I should say scrubbing, her toenails with his toothbrush!

At least Charlie was man enough, first to throw her out without any payment, but also to share his humiliation with his mates.

Departure date drew closer and the invitations to farewell lunches and dinner poured in. One for lunch that will remain forever memorable came from a businessman, who had from the outset been most helpful to me, a relationship that developed beyond that of simply a business nature.

'John,' he said, 'before you leave I want to invite you to a special lunch at one of my favourite restaurants.'

The day came and off we set in his car. Down this side street, up the next, till we stepped out to a row of buildings with no obvious eatery visible. On opening a plain unsigned door we entered a small foyer from which a long steep stairway led seemingly forever upwards. All the way up were fish tanks filled with live fish, prawns, crabs and other forms of seafood. Clearly a fish restaurant. Ushered to a privately situated table by a bevy of waiters, who clearly knew and paid obvious homage to my host, we prepared to begin what turned out to be a feast.

Nothing unusual I can feel you thinking. Oh yes, what an experience this luncheon turned out to be. Ten courses and each one 'alive!'. Not one dish was presented other than *au natural*! Starting with mussels, then cockles, then baby shrimp, then larger shrimp. Fresh seaweeds were followed by sashimi prepared at the table, the flapping fish looking at you bright eyed, mouth gasping for breath before the skilled hand of the chef deftly sliced and then diced a choice fillet, the pieces then being delicately arranged for one to pick up with chopsticks. After almost two hours we left having consumed a large quantity of rice wine (sake) and I feeling decidedly like a well-satisfied cannibal.

Although relatively brief, our time in Taiwan was a demanding but happy period for the family. David was flourishing and we met many expatriates from the private sector, representing their companies, being posted and living in Taipei, who became close friends.

A mountainous country, only one-third being of cultivable land, but in many parts very beautiful. In spring the blossoms from the many species planted throughout the hills surrounding Taipei were spectacular. Rhododendrons, camellias, plum and cherry trees, all introduced by the Japanese during their fifty year occupation (1895–1945).

One cannot leave this chapter of our life without mention of the Central Museum of Taipei which houses an incredible collection of Chinese art (paintings, scrolls, bronzes, jade and wooden and ivory carvings). If a visitor only does one thing when in Taiwan, a visit to the Museum is mandatory.

We were sorry to leave, but to those interested in the fortunes and misfortunes of the people of this beautiful island from the 1940s, I would strongly recommend George H. Kerr's *Formosa Betrayed*, first published by Eyre and Spottiswoode Ltd, London, in 1966.

The Manager's Residence, Muar River Estate, Batu Anam Johore, Malaya, where I spent the first seven years of my life. Above, front view, below, the dining room side.

Standing outside a bathing box with Bruce Andrews (right) at Seacliff beach, Adelaide, 1947.

The Hon. R.G. (Bob) Menzies, in transit at Calcutta, on the way to London to attend the Commonwealth Heads of Government Meeting, midnight, 24 May 1962.

Professor Paul Engle, of Iowa State University, and author visiting the Ajanta Caves, India.

Within the grounds of the Shwedagon Pagoda, Yangon (Rangoon), Myanmar (Burma).

Maureen riding a camel, visiting the Cheops Pyramid and the Sphinx, Cairo, Egypt.

At the Colossi of Memnon, Thebes, Egypt.

A guide on a felucca.

Feluccas on the Nile.

The port of Aden, Yemen.

A dhow under construction in Ma'alla, Aden.

Wedding day! St David's Church, Lindfield, NSW. 24 January, 1966.

Our much-loved 'Knutsford of Millbrook', Hong Kong, 1966.

Maureen and Joe (my father) enjoy a day out on the harbour, Hong Kong, 1966.

Waiting to receive guests, Australia Day, 26 January 1966, Hong Kong.

Maureen with David Anthony, whilst we were on leave in Sydney, 1967, before proceeding to Taipei, Taiwan.

The official opening of the Australian Trade Commissioner's Office by the Economic Minister, Mr K.T. Li, Taipei, Taiwan in early 1968.

Queen Elizabeth visits Bangkok. David (far left) has just greeted Her Majesty.

Conducting H.E. Minister Pate Sarasin, Minister of National Development, around the Australian Trade Display after he had officially opened the display. Bangkok, 1972.

On the occasion of presentation to His Majesty the King of Thailand of an Australian-made aircraft, the Airtruk, purchased by the Ministry of Agriculture.

His Majesty The King of Thailand, Minister 'Salty' Sellars, Australian Embassy, Bangkok, and the author.

A group photo in front of the Airtruk. Built by Transavia, the Airtruk was an agricultural aircraft.

Our weekend retreat at Memillon, France whilst stationed in Paris, 1974–1979.
I sketched the house in 1975.

President Suharto of Indonesia, at a barbecue he hosted at his farm in the Puncak area, Indonesia, December 1982.

With 'Sam' at Friedrichsdorf (near Frankfurt), West Germany, 1989.

The 'G10', the ten Executive General Managers of Austrade, June 1993.
Back row (left to right): Peter Langhorne, John Allgrove, Charlie Jamieson (dec.), Peter Forsythe, Michael Johnson, Dieter LeComte (dec.)
Front row (left to right): David Oliver, Ralph Evans (MD), Peter Cook (Minister for Trade in the Keating Government), Bill Ferris (Chairman), Alex Stuart, Greg Dodds
Absent: Paul Twomey

At the 'Old Blues' luncheon, Adelaide, 4 October 2012.

At the Ionian Club Convention Cocktail Party, Crowne Plaza Hotel, Adelaide, 2 May 2014.
With us (left) is Liz Scarce, the wife of the (then) Governor of South Australia,
Rear Admiral Kevin Scarce.

Happily retired, after 34 years' service.

CHAPTER FIVE

Bangkok, Thailand

1970–1973

Post included responsibilities for Australia's trade interests in Thailand, Burma (Myanmar), Vietnam, Cambodia and Laos.

Taking place mid career, Bangkok was to be a defining point in our life, the place we experienced the tragic loss of our eldest son David on 21 January 1973, following a fall in the schoolyard a few days earlier. The heart-wrenching decision that we made to have his life support system turned off will be forever with us both. A fall, a bump on the forehead, the ensuing lump 'going in' instead of out resulting in a 'brain-dead' condition.

David would have turned six on 4 April, just a couple of months later.

However, a miracle had preceded this very personal tragedy. Marc was born on 23 October 1971, and was just fifteen months old when David died.

We forced ourselves to move on, cherishing memories and photos and throwing ourselves even more into caring for Anne-Marie and Marc. Having the two of them helped us so much with the busy lives we led, both professionally and socially.

One feature of this very difficult period that I would like to record, was the extraordinary loyalty of Sam, my office driver. Though one of the pool of drivers, Sam spent the greater part of his day driving for me and the trade section of the Embassy. Sam insisted that over this period of four to five days neither I nor Maureen would drive ourselves. For no extra pay, he slept in our car, ready whenever needed, twenty-four hours a day.

We shall never forget you Sam.

Although very different from Taiwan, from whence we had just come, it was just as important to understand Thailand's history, unique in the whole of Asia. Among its particular characteristics was the role of women. A powerful influence in the home and in business. Perhaps nothing demonstrates this more to a foreigner than if a foreigner marries a Thai woman and returns to his own country, as most expatriates do, then ultimately their Thai wife will take them back to her homeland to live. Maybe not quite so prevalent in this the 21st century of easy travel and instant communications, but certainly during our time as residents of this full-of-interest country.

Following the Mon/Khmer/Thai Wars the Burmese sacked Ayutthaya in 1767, following which the Thais then defeated the Burmese. Bangkok has been the capital since 1782 when King Rama I became the first king of the present Chakri Dynasty. Since then brilliant diplomacy kept Western powers at bay, to the extent that to this day there has been no colonisation of Thailand. (Compare British colonisation of India, Burma, Malaya, Ceylon; French of Laos, Vietnam and Cambodia; Dutch of Indonesia, to name a few in the region.)

Cleverly managed politics has resulted in not infrequent 'disturbances' be they factional or racial, being settled amicably. Multiple coups have been bloodless. 'As the wind blows, so the bamboo bends', describes the Thai temperament perfectly. One has but to compare similar disturbances between ethnic Chinese and Malays in Malaysia or Chinese and Indonesians in Indonesia, the latter being particularly violent at the end of the President Sukarno period.

Overall, the overriding impression we gained of Thai society during our four-year posting was that of a harsh lesson in priorities. Family is all important, with its interacting relationships and their contributions to society being more important than material possessions.

As already indicated, territory responsibility for the Bangkok post included Laos, Vietnam, Cambodia and Burma (Myanmar). The three former French colonies I visited more frequently between 1991–1995 when responsible for the South-East Asia region as executive general manager. The regime in Burma made visiting as a holder of a diplomatic passport difficult given the then policy of the Australian Government, but fortunately I had previously enjoyed the experience when posted in Calcutta during my first assignment in the TC Service. Great people and memorable experiences including many visits to the Shwedagon Pagoda in Rangoon (Yangon), Mandalay to the north and the, even today, not to be missed multitude of pagodas, small and large, stretching as far as the eye can see across the plains in Pagan.

On arriving in Bangkok in 1970 with two young children, David three years, Anne-Marie barely two, our first nights were spent at the Erawan Hotel, sadly now no longer there. An elegant building of Thai-style architecture in structure and close to where we were to live. Enjoying the hotel pool over the first weekend, we were confronted by a woman bent over the side of the pool. She had noticed that given we were a family, it was likely we weren't tourists, but that we were coming to Bangkok on a posting for some foreign company, government or NGO. Upon receiving confirmation that this was the case, she simply stated that we obviously would wish to have a dog. It was the last thing on our mind at the time, but we soon weakened to the children, insisting that we would. So it came to pass that soon after we moved into Soi Langsuan, Pepper – a crossbreed several times over – was delivered.

Next door was the residence of the Austrian Ambassador, whose shitzu-type canine, though relatively small, was still larger in the early days than Pepper, and frequently came into our compound, soiled our lawn, and terrorised Pepper. Soon, however, their relative sizes changed and one day, before our eyes, Pepper had clearly had enough, and went for his hated antagonist. Through the dividing hedge, across neighbouring foreign diplomatic territory, and into the Austrian

Ambassador's residence the chase continued, until Pepper caught his previous nemesis, opening up his belly skin with one deft lurch. Oh dear! How bloodstained was the carpet! Diplomatic relations were soured to say the least, but in our view – and certainly Pepper's – justice had at last been done.

Sadly Pepper grew to alsatian proportions and couldn't be trusted with children or other dogs, and instead became a guard dog for a well-heeled Thai family.

He was replaced with our beloved Baggins, a boxer – the breed now becoming a firm favourite in the Allgrove household.

In the life we led, postings of three to four years always presented a problem when one left as to what to do with pets. This was usually solved by giving them to one's successor or a friend made during time spent in the country. Baggins found a good home in this way.

Bangkok was often referred to then as the Venice of the East because of its vast network of *klongs* (waterways) stretching as roads for kilometres, and extensively used for transporting goods in barges, and people in longtail boats. Along their banks were located endless homes, either on stilts or floating, which provided the backdrop for what was a constantly moving mass of people and goods – perhaps the most well-known and colourful being the floating markets. Sadly many *klongs* have been filled in and converted into roads, with resulting floods being more prevalent in the wet season.

Visits out of Bangkok were relatively infrequent as most contacts for Australian exporters were located within the city. For personal reasons, however, there is much to see and do in the country. North to Chiang Mai and Chiang Rai, the old city of Ayutthaya a must. Lazy day on the Chao Phraya River, which runs through Bangkok giving constant riverbank images of old temples and confirming how closely related Thais are with the water.

For relief from the heat and bustle of Bangkok we looked forward to regular visits to Pattaya, the coastal holiday resort south of the city where the Embassy had several cottages available for Australian-based families to use on a roster system. Those having young children keenly anticipated the availability of these.

Of more sombre interest were visits to Kanchanaburi, the location of the bridge over the River Kwai. Many visitors wished to see where the first prisoner of war camps were located as they, as slave labour, set out to build a railway from Thailand to Burma. Many will have seen the film of the same name.

Of such personal relevance was the fact that my father, a rubber planter in Malaysia, spent World War Two as a POW of the Japanese engaged on this infamous venture. So many Europeans, Chinese, Indian and Thai nationals perished at this time.

Dad survived and stayed on in Malaysia and Singapore for some three months after his release at the end of the Pacific War (16 August 1945) to try and find Mother or what happened to her, before coming to Adelaide to meet up (he hoped!) with my sister Jane and me.

National parks were great venues for a Sunday picnic, a swim in a rockpool, and to take in the abundant wildlife.

One very un-Thai rural business was that of the Chokchai Ranch Co. Ltd, the managing director of which was one amazing character, Chokchai Bulkul, who had spent years in the US learning the ways of raising cattle on American-style ranches. He came back to Thailand and established his ranch, which mirrored in every way that of the American model. Cowboys, horses, boots, saddles, the lot.

I wanted this story of initially my, and then our (Maureen and my), life to be largely that of humorous and other experiences, to be readable and hopefully interesting, and in no way a factual account of Australia's trade efforts in the regions to which I had been posted, and perhaps the part that I may have played in advancing the interests of Australian companies. I leave that to historians to compile. A document of that nature finds its place in a library, and other than for perhaps a few, is frankly boring.

And so to 'Stories from Thailand'. As community service director of the Rotary Club of Bangkok South, my responsibilities included arranging a major fundraising event each year. 'Why not be really ambitious,' suggested a colleague, 'and bring the Surin Elephants to Bangkok?' These, some fifty or so, spend most of the year working in the teak forests in northern Thailand, each with their own *mahout*. During the wet season however, they come south to Surin situated some 300 kilometres north-east of Bangkok, where they become a major tourist attraction giving performances of their many skills, such as simulated Burmese-Thai battles of years gone by, moving logs, performing egg and spoon races. Contact was made with the head *mahout*, who came to Bangkok to discuss the proposal. This meeting took place, as did many subsequent meetings, in a private room at the Oriental Hotel, at that time, and probably still today, regarded as one of the five star plus hotels in the world. One has to picture five or so Rotarians in business dress, and one very weather-worn singlet- and short-clad *mahout* in his fifties, who clearly had spent most of his life exposed to the elements.

Gradually plans fell into place, but soon the magnitude of the task became apparent. We pushed ahead, determined to pursue such an ambitious, but exciting, project.

Moving so many elephants, walking a limited number of kilometres per day from Surin to Bangkok and return, over several weeks, meant that some ten or more staging points had to be prepared. The space to tether these pachyderms had first to be found. Then ensuring there was sufficient water, bunches of bananas and palm fronds for food. Each *mahout* had to be looked after. Costs were mounting.

The final meeting began and all the boxes were ticked one by one until the head *mahout* said, 'You have forgotten one thing.' We looked at each other in a surprised and questioning manner. Before we could even enquire, he said, 'You have forgotten what you are going to do with the shit while the elephants are in one place in Bangkok for up to two weeks!' Jaws dropping, we burst into laughter, but almost before we could accept that this was going to be a major problem, one club member, who ran a large orchid-growing enterprise, offered to 'take the lot'.

The whole exercise was, as far as the show was concerned, a great and colourful success, all of which I captured on film, but one must admit, a financial failure. We didn't lose money, but we failed to make any.

But what a club team effort. One member provided the area to hold performances, another the stands, another the bananas, palm fronds, sugar cane, another the water trucks, another the publicity and ticketing arrangements and, yes, thankfully one to cart away all the shit!

One lovely final touch was that one of the herd produced a baby whilst in Bangkok, which became a great attraction when word got round. The troupe returned happily to Surin with one extra family member.

Hard to imagine in a city with Bangkok's climate, but one of the many evenings we enjoyed the most was having a sauna followed by dinner at the home of Esko and Anja Pajasalmi, a Finnish family. Esko was managing director of Presko Public Relations Co. Ltd, which handled all our public relations work for trade fairs or for the needs of an individual Australian exporter. Esko imported a complete sauna room from Finland to provide complete authenticity to the process, including the volcanic stones and their stove, which when heated were doused with water to provide the necessary steam to ensure a good sweat! We would then throw pails of ice-cold water over ourselves, followed by cooling off in an air-conditioned room dressed in gowns, and lounging on rugs and pillows whilst downing more than one vodka. Altogether a trifle decadent!

Then came dinner of Finnish delicacies including various processed fish and sausages, cheeses washed down, with care, with more Finnish vodka. One slept really well after such an evening.

Of concern and excitement, and some danger, occurred when a group of Black September terrorists took over the Israeli Embassy/Ambassador's residence, which was situated two houses along from our home. The street was sealed off and for several days was swarming with soldiers, police and negotiating officials. ABC reporters anxious to file reports spent long hours in our lounge and patio area given not only our proximity to the action, but having the only nearby phone line. The phone bill soared, as did the consumption of Aussie beer, particularly Foster's Lager and Victoria Bitter. Sandwiches were also in constant demand. Finally in Thai style a peaceful withdrawal was negotiated.

The King's Birthday in December was a yearly event of great importance and celebration, with one massive audience given by His Majesty in the palace for officials and the diplomatic corps. This, if one was invited, was a command performance which required long gowns for ladies and tails and white tie for men. It was the only opportunity that one had of entering the inner sanctums of the palace, Emerald Buddha included.

The major drawback however was the stifling heat, exacerbated by the restrictions of dress. One dripped with perspiration the whole time, particularly as the main halls of the palace were not air-conditioned. We endured this 'must attend' wonderfully colourful event three times, and lost weight on each occasion!

There are many tales to tell of the antics that numerous businessmen got up to whilst in Bangkok, but I'll refrain from telling tales except for one that took place during the visit of a significant trade mission to Thailand, and provided great amusement at the daily briefing for mission members.

Following an official function the previous evening, the said individual decided to take a ride in a long-tail boat on the Chao Phraya River, setting forth from the well-known pick-up point near the Oriental Hotel. During a general meander along the canals in the vicinity of the floating markets, he heard the cry of a dog. Being an avid RSPCA supporter he immediately sensed cruelty and asked the boatman to pull into the nearest landing. Stepping ashore he advanced purposely to a door from which shone a light into the otherwise dark night. At that point a small dog was ejected on the end of a swift kick.

Incensed, he confronted the individual and said that cruelty of this nature to an animal was not to be tolerated – all expressed in English to an individual who only spoke Thai. Anyway, the latter managed to convey that if this part-crazy white man felt so strongly, he could take the dog. Incredibly he did. Picking up the dog, which was not much more than a puppy, he reached the water's edge when, not wishing to be taken from its home – kick or no kick – the dog bit our Aussie mission member on the face. The dog was dropped and immediately ran back to its owner, which one suspects he knew it would.

Bleeding and with fears of a possible rabies infection, a hasty return to the hotel, now close to midnight, was made.

Only next morning, swathed in bandages, he entered the briefing meeting and the story finally came out. You can imagine the comments; 'A dog, c'mon, why didn't she like you?' etc., etc. With a damaged face one feels for the explanations that were attempted when he got back home.

Perhaps my favourite story occurred during an official visit to Thailand of Queen Elizabeth, Prince Philip and Princess Anne. One significant event in the programme was that given by the British Ambassador in the late afternoon on the spacious back lawns of the splendid, very colonial-like, residence. Organised so the Royals could meet representatives of Commonwealth countries stationed in Thailand, each group of thirty or so were assembled in country groups, beginning with Australians on the left, followed by Canadians, concluding with representatives of New Zealand on the right – all countries arranged in a semicircle fanned out from the steps to the lawn from the residence.

Her Majesty, Philip and Anne each started meeting groups separately, moving around so that at any one time only one was with each group.

At this stage I must explain that I was wearing a Trans Australia Airline (TAA) tie, dark blue with the emblem of a stylised flying kangaroo resting on a spear. Now no longer an airline, it was at that time the internal carrier of the federal government. Though a kangaroo, the design was different from the well-known Qantas emblem. I was confronted by the Duke of Edinburgh, accompanied by the Australian Ambassador, Tom Critchley. The Duke didn't wait for Tom to introduce me as to what was my position within the Embassy, namely Minister Commercial and Senior Trade Commissioner, but asked, 'And how long have you been representing Qantas in Thailand?' I quickly thought that one cannot complicate matters by pointing out that the Duke was wrong and then trying to unravel the exchange, so simply replied, 'Three years, your Highness.' 'And during that time what has been the increase in passenger and freight loadings?' 'Eight and twelve per cent respectively, sir.'

Prince Philip moved on down the Australian line.

Towards the end he asked of one of us, 'And what are you doing in Thailand?'

'I am the manager of Qantas, sir.'

'No you're not. I've just met the manager of Qantas up there,' pointing in my direction.

The individual was indeed the manager of Qantas and understandably embarrassed at being called a liar! It cost me a few beers at the end of the day.

The King's interest in the use of aerial seeding of clouds to produce rain provided the opportunity of meeting His Majesty on more than one occasion, the most memorable being when the Ministry of Agriculture purchased one of Transavia's (part of the Transfield group of companies) Airtruks. The handing over ceremony, attended by the King, took place in Hua Hin, south along the Thai peninsula towards Malaysia, where the King had one of his retreats. Garlands, blessings and many senior officials prostrating themselves (not required of foreign officials) before His Majesty made for a colourful ceremony, though for me a little embarrassing, when a Thai minister approached the King in a crawling posture, while I simply shook his hand as we would normally greet anyone.

We learned to love the Thai people and were sad to leave when the time came, but leave we had to after four very happy years – though obviously desperately sad when we lost David.

Before leaving, Maureen and I were asleep in the early morning when Canberra called – not known for recognising time differences – and a well-known voice asked, 'Do you know of the Eiffel Tower, and would you like to see it?' An odd, but exciting way of saying, 'Your next posting is Paris, France.'

So with that knowledge we left Thailand carrying David's ashes with us on our lap in the aircraft. Soon after we arranged for the urn to be interred in the grounds of St David's Presbyterian Church, Lindfield, Sydney, NSW. We had been married at St David's and all the children subsequently baptised there. We arranged for the area between the vestry and front door entrances – a triangular area next to the Pacific Highway – to be paved and a white camellia planted. David's urn lies beneath the camellia.

CHAPTER SIX

Paris, France

1974–1979

Post included responsibilities for Australia's trade interests in Tunisia, Algeria, Morocco and during first year of posting, Spain.

What was to be our longest posting in my career began with a period of two months language training. Arriving early in 1974, the whole family flew via London to Nice, and thence to Villefranche-sur-Mer – a delightful fishing village situated between Nice and Monaco. With boats bobbing in the harbour on one side and snow-capped mountains on the other, it really was a picture post-card location.

The management of the school found a comfortable apartment for us, as well as a babysitter for Anne-Marie and Marc, by now five and two respectively. A Polish lady – a very accomplished basketball player – arrived at our front door the day after we settled in. Maureen opened the door and what confronted her initially created fear in the children, who hid behind their mother's skirts. At over 6'5" she represented someone to be respected. Turning out to be a gem we – and the children – grew to love, respect and certainly trust to look after the young ones during the day while we were both away.

The school was within walking distance and our day began with breakfast at eight followed by classes, lunch, more classes and concluding with afternoon tea at four. The children were very pleased to see us come home. Five days a week of this regime for such an extended period really tested their patience.

Weekends saw us hiring a Renault 5 and touring the hinterland, visiting villages for lunch, and inspecting craft shops and galleries of which there were many. One favourite was Èze, a picturesque cliff-top village with fortified walls and cobblestone streets. Choosing a luncheon venue we took our seats and ordered. Then we waited. Not such a problem for Maureen and me, but testing for the children. We queried the length of time for our meals to arrive and received what we came to expect, a cool shrug as if to say, 'This is France, and what's more it's the weekend.' In France you eat out to enjoy the atmosphere, the food, and to do this you stretch the process out. Okay, but it became too much when the food for the dogs of those at the adjoining table came before ours!

Visits to Monaco and Nice were frequent, changing of the guard at the palace in the former and the gardens being memorable. We didn't try our luck at the casino, having the children with us being a reasonable excuse, apart from the fact we couldn't afford to lose. As part of the course, we had several evenings out for dinner – all conversation had to be in French – and one colourful night saw us in a restaurant where all the waiters conducted their craft on rollerskates at high speed. Later in the evening they put on a brilliant musical floor show, before again tending to customers at their tables.

One must note however that these famous southern coast of France towns had one great deficiency and that was that what they regarded as beaches we saw for what they really were – just a stretch of rocks and pebbles. Most uninviting!

At the conclusion of our course we moved to Paris to begin our life in earnest, work, and school for the children. Our first few nights were spent at the Hilton Hotel situated on the other side of the Champs de Mars from where our apartment was situated. In between was the Eiffel Tower.

After bedding the children down we prepared for our first dinner in Paris and our first experience of French pig-headedness! We both ordered, in Australian-accented but correct, French, a seafood entree followed by Beef Wellington – *boeuf en croûte*! Lingering a little over our white wine with entree finished, we requested that our ordered

red be served. No action, no reaction. Pregnant pause saw our request repeated. After five to ten minutes we insisted. The sommelier's reaction was equally tense, 'Sir, I will not serve the red until you have finished your white wine!' No problem, we met his request and learnt from the experience.

On another occasion a colleague and his wife were visiting from London. An evening in one of our favourite restaurants saw our guests order a well-done steak. 'Sorry, sir, in France we prepare steak rare, pink or medium. If another guest saw you consuming a well-done steak, they would never return to our restaurant.'

Within a day or so, when our household effects were delivered, we moved to our apartment on the corner of Avenue de la Bourdonnais, a stone's throw from the Eiffel Tower. Also situated within walking distance of the Embassy located, at that time, in Avenue d'Iéna at the Arc de Triomphe end of d'Iéna. A very pleasant twenty minute morning's exercise across the River Seine. Traffic constantly moving on the river- and tree-lined streets bordering so many wonderful buildings, made the start of the day such a pleasurable one.

With so much to see and do, even if it was sitting on the footpath enjoying a coffee and witnessing the passing parade between deciding what was next on the agenda, life was forever full. The children attended the École Active Bilingue, an English/French bilingual school, although somewhat a misnomer, because most of the day was conducted entirely in the French language. The most important legacy of their experience was that they 'learned how to learn'. How valuable this was to become apparent in later years at Years 11 and 12 and university.

The one thing neither children nor we could get used to was a particular aspect of French medical practice. For children, seldom was a pill to be swallowed; prescribed was a suppository. Try convincing a young boy to bend over and accept a pill up his you-know-where! How degrading, how humiliating, how disgusting!

In the immediate vicinity of where we lived were restaurants and cafes in abundance, weekly markets offering the freshest of meat, vegetables and cheeses. Bread, especially the much consumed baguette, was baked continually. For breakfast one went out to purchase early in the morning. If one was entertaining and wanted fresh baguettes for lunch or dinner, one made the purchase an hour or so before, not any earlier. Then if a very special treat was required there was Poilâne bakery around the corner. Legendary wood-oven-baked bread is exported around the world by air daily from Poilâne's, especially to New York.

The new Embassy and accommodation complex were constructed during our stay, situated just the other side of the Champs de Mars from where we lived. Designed by architect extraordinaire Harry Seidler, we were the first family to take up residence in this most modern of accommodation. All apartments designed to house various levels of officers from secretaries to ambassador had their public area and balcony facing the Seine, and all bedrooms looked out over the chimney-covered rooftops of the city. Brilliant. Several levels of car parking beneath, as well as a squash court, swimming pool and the room for all electricals – all below flood level, which was later to prove a disaster. More on that later.

Harry was, however, the most egotistical person I have ever met – besotted with his own genius. When his creation was complete there came the day when the Embassy transferred from Avenue d'Iéna, all accomplished over one weekend. On the Monday morning we all arrived for the first day! It was not long before I heard loud shouting coming from the office of one of my senior staff, who had chosen to move his desk slightly so that when seated the Eiffel Tower was framed in the window. Harry was wandering around, happened to notice this and issued a vigorous reprimand, 'How dare you rearrange furniture that I personally have positioned.' Needless to say the said staff member was aghast and reacted accordingly. It took more than a little of my diplomatic skills to keep the two physically apart. Unbelievable. One should point out that Harry had been given the contract to design and furnish the Embassy and accommodation buildings, including choice of furniture and floor coverings, even ashtrays! He took it upon himself to include the positioning of *every* item. In the Ambassador's quarters to be occupied by the Ambassador to the OECD, one Pat Donovan, Harry insisted in positioning all paintings and refusing the hanging of some of Pat and Maria's own collection, which included a number of valuable pieces and icons from tsarist Russia.

A fireplace, never to be used, but nevertheless a feature of the main public area of the Donovan residence, was filled with logs from the forests surrounding Paris – each personally selected by Harry.

Some months after completion, Harry – accompanied by Max Dupain, the renowned architectural photographer – arrived to gather material for the production of *Harry Seidler, Australian Embassy, Ambassade d'Australie, Paris*, a comprehensive photographic and engineering explanatory document. A number of branches of a tree situated on the boulevard along the banks of the Seine obscured the optimum frontal photo so they were removed using a chainsaw! A well produced publication and a nice memento, having been posted in Paris, but the cheek of such an action taken without any request being lodged or necessary subsequent approval being obtained from the office of the Mayor of Paris.

Working life was not easy. The UK had only recently joined the Common Market and Australia's exports of primary products to the EEC immediately became less attractive to consumers because of quantity and duty restrictions. Just one example of French stubbornness in being even slightly reasonable follows.

Exports of buffalo meat to the EEC from the Northern Territory represented the livelihood of a significant number of people, with the principal market being, at that time, West Germany. Beef production in the EEC encouraged by massive subsidies outgrew consumption, resulting in huge stockpiles – as was the case with butter and a number of other agricultural products. What to do? Stocks had to be cleared. Warehouses were overflowing. In step the clever Russians. In need of beef to feed their people, they waited until the Western European stockpile crisis reached the point when they knew almost any offer would be accepted as it always was, resulting in a huge loss to EEC governments.

The French in trying to mitigate the problem decided that buffalo meat, though regarded hitherto as a game meat incurring little or no duty, should be classified as beef and were able to persuade their Common Market colleagues that this should be so. Overnight orders already prepared for shipment from the NT were cancelled.

For several weeks I strode the corridors of the French Ministry of Agriculture arguing that these shipments be allowed to enter under the former regime for various reasons: commercial honesty, recognition of the financial hardship that would be inflicted on about 150 Australian families involved in all stages of the trade, and perhaps so as to avoid spoiling France's reputation as a responsible nation with which to do business.

The principal official I dealt with was the head of the ministry's meat division, a M. Piquet. Puffy face, small glasses and beady eyes would look at me over his heavy French-oak desk in a high-ceiling office with Saint Gobain glass chandeliers and the odd Gobelin tapestry adorning the walls. For style one could not match the French.

Finally the day came when I pushed aside the almost daily cables (no computers and emails in those days) that contained communiques from the Australian government that I should present – all in firm but nevertheless diplomatic language – and said in a very strong voice, 'Monsieur Piquet, you and your government are being completely unreasonable and show an unacceptable recognition of the hardship that your action will inflict on some 150 Australian families.'

M. Piquet looked straight at me and replied, 'Monsieur Minister Commercial, I don't care what happens to 150 Australian families.' My hands tightened on the edge of his desk and, fortunately for the individual facing me, it was far too heavy for me to move. The nearest

I ever came in my career to causing a diplomatic incident. I said my farewell and stormed out of his office!

But there were many more happy occasions, one being when I arranged an ambassadorial visit to the south of France, principally to Marseilles, one of the great ports of the world with a long, long history. My interlocutor was one M. Yann-Pierre Remond, director of the Port Authority of Marseilles. Many phone calls were exchanged in French, mine with difficulty, but I persevered. Finally the day came when a large DS23 Citroën collected the Ambassador and me from our hotel, we having flown down the previous evening from Paris, and we were escorted to M. Remond's office, once again decorated in lavish style.

I had never met M. Remond before, but confidently advanced and, in reasonable French, greeted him, thanked him for receiving us, for arrangements made and of course introducing the ambassador, who incidentally spoke perfect French. Before either of us could utter a word, from the mouth of M. Remond came, 'G'day, mate, good to see ya!' My reaction was uncontrollably instantaneous, 'You bastard!' We all collapsed in laughter, though some of his staff were stunned. M. Yann-Pierre Remond spent his early years in Sydney (his father was with BNP bank, or maybe in the wool business, and Y-P went to Cranbrook). By the time the family returned to Paris, Y-P knew all about throwing another shrimp on the barbie! He did apologise for what he put me through, but justified his actions by saying that it helped me with my French! Incidentally, we still exchange yearly greetings, Christmas cards that Y-P paints himself, and he and his charming wife Christiane have visited us here in Adelaide.

Never to be forgotten was the visit of Prime Minister Malcolm Fraser to France. A major emphasis involved trade matters, nuclear industry issues, as well as the supply of defence equipment. My main contribution to the PM's schedule was to arrange the guest list for a luncheon at the ambassador's residence for some twenty of France's most senior bankers and industrialists. Fortunately I had been at my assignment long enough to make the list a reasonably easy task. I could speak to each personally.

The PM and his large party arrived early one morning and the motorcade sped (with police escort) directly to the Hotel de Crillon situated on the corner of Place de la Concorde, a large square at the bottom of Avenue des Champs-Élysées in the centre of which stands Cleopatra's Needle.

Lunch was scheduled for 1 pm and I was assigned the task of accompanying the PM from the hotel to the ambassador's residence. At this point one should point out that PM's schedules were planned to the minute and this occasion called for me to be outside the PM's room at 12.40 pm. PM would appear at 12.45 pm and be escorted downstairs to his car, all other members of his party attending the lunch to already be in their cars – a whole line of black DS23 Citroëns. The police escort would lead the motorcade off, once the PM, and I, were in his vehicle and belted up.

On arrival on the footpath in front of the hotel, with French driver holding the door open for the PM – I had already ascertained which side he wished to travel – Prime Minister Fraser turned to me and said, 'I want to go in that car,' pointing to a stretched limousine parked some fifty metres away to the right. It happened to be the French press vehicle!

I had long ago learned that one doesn't argue with the PM, at least not this one. Signalling to the Embassy staff member in charge of our cars, I instructed him to find the driver. Hesitancy at first turned quickly to action (he could see I wasn't to be argued with either), and we moved towards the vehicle of choice, took our seats in the rear and took off.

Having a lot of leg room, the PM, a very tall man, stretched out and asked, 'Where are these Mercedes vehicles converted to one like this?'

'I'm afraid I don't know, PM, but I'll find out immediately after lunch.'

Next question.

'What are the torque problems that are faced because of the extended tail shaft from gearbox to differential?' Same response from me.

'Oh, and why isn't my official flag flying from the front mudguard?'

'Because, PM, it's not your bloody car!'

'Fair enough, but make sure it is when we return following lunch.'

The journey from hotel to the Ambassador's residence, a very gracious French chateau-style building, took about ten minutes. I had prepared answers to some of the trade-related questions that I thought the PM may realistically ask of his Minister Commercial/Senior Trade Commissioner in Paris. There were many issues. Ask any of them? Not one!

On arrival I escorted the PM to the rear garden where guests were assembling. The Ambassador had asked me to stay close to him to make sure he got names and occupations right as each guest arrived. No way, I had to find a phone and call the operational nerve centre at the hotel and arrange for the PM's flag to be fitted to the car!

Lunch passed without incident and when the PM and I emerged to the courtyard a quick look eased any anxiety I may have had, as there was the flag! The only remark uttered by the PM on the return journey was, 'Thank you for fixing the flag.' Oh dear! How wrong one can be when trying to prioritise matters of importance!

It's worth pointing out that the staff to which the flag was attached was an egg slice from the kitchen jammed between the bonnet and engine compartment. On a bit of an angle, but when moving the flag fluttered beautifully!

Probably the most memorable visit paid during my whole posting was accompanying the then Minister of Trade, Doug Anthony, and party to the south of France, followed by nuclear establishments in Tricastin and then Cap de la Hague (not Le Havre), where the French facility for reprocessing of spent uranium rods was situated. More of that later.

To begin, the target was a small town called Mazamet – the heart of the fellmongering industry in Europe. Sheepskins treated here came almost entirely from Australia. One particular company had strong long-time relations with Australia, having an office in Melbourne for many years – namely Rives P.H. Pty Ltd. Another important player was the French bank, Banque Nationale de Paris (BNP). Well before stricter regulations were introduced, BNP opened a branch in Australia just to facilitate the business of sheepskin sales to France. It is a business based on very fine margins and exchanges (cable traffic at the time) occurred each day. A representative from the office of Rives P.H. in Melbourne would be in attendance at the main municipal abattoir each morning to buy sheepskins, a by-product of the sheep meat trade. Prices were relayed to head office in Mazamet and instructions given to buy or otherwise. Cables received in Mazamet on Monday morning concluded, during the football (Australian Rules) season, with Saturday's results. For many years, sheepskin exports to France represented the most significant item by value – by a large margin.

Interestingly however, there had never been a visit to Mazamet by an Australian Government Minister, whilst in office, to this small town in the south of France. It was situated where there was an abundant supply of pure water so necessary for the process, particularly that of the follow-up industry, namely the production of chamois leather from the skins after the wool had been removed. This I felt important to change and Doug Anthony readily agreed.

We arrived by train in Toulouse and were met by a fleet of cars and later joined by a police motorcade at the provincial border and escorted into Mazamet. The welcome was amazing. Police, fire brigade vehicles, local officials led by the mayor and almost everyone who thought he or she should be there. Whilst the main reception in the Town Hall was lavish, nothing proved as moving as the private dinner at the country estate of Mr Philip Rives himself, by then in his late eighties or more, and retired. A sumptuous meal, everything from the farm itself, was accompanied by superb wines, one of which was the remaining red wine served at the wedding of Mr and Mrs Rives, some sixty years before. The wine was probably fifteen to twenty years old then, so we were treated to something very special.

Next stop represented a mega leap forward insofar as the comparison of industries was involved. We visited the heart of the French nuclear energy electricity production industry, Tricastin. Tall, square-walled buildings next to large bottle-shaped cooling towers, each emitting volumes of steam. An industry situated in the heart of one of France's many wine producing regions – in fact the home of more than a reasonable drop of red, namely, Châteauneuf-du-Pape. The French have done a remarkable job in 'selling' the use of nuclear power to produce electricity to its electorate. Everyone we spoke to expressed no concern in living, working and consuming agricultural products, all within the immediate proximity of a nuclear establishment. This was emphasised in the most persuasive way when we later visited Cap de la Hague on the far west coast of the country. An Alcatraz Prison-looking structure from the outside. From the top one looks straight down to the sea on the western side and equally straight down to green pastures that grow right up to the walls on the eastern. These pastures supported cows, all happily grazing, from the milk of which is produced the world famous camembert cheese.

A personal opinion, but I do believe that to ultimately satisfy the world's energy needs, nuclear power will be the only choice – at least to produce the base load required. Burning coal and oil contribute too much to climate change and ultimately supplies will run out or be too expensive to retrieve. Solar, wind and wave technology – though clearly able to contribute – will not keep up with the requirements of an ever-increasing population and the desire of so many Third World economies wishing to enjoy the benefits so long taken for granted by the Western world.

Many often ask, 'Of all your postings, which one have you and the family most enjoyed?' Must be responded to in two ways. From one's own work aspect, France was the least pleasant. I met many who have become loyal friends, but each day there was always the barrier of the Common Market Policy to be dealt with and, as already indicated, usually with very difficult officials.

However, as a total experience, Paris would certainly be our favourite. The city itself is magic, the countryside unbelievable. Always beauty to behold, structures dating back to the Middle Ages to admire and superb food to enjoy in quaint country towns. We tried most of the forays recommended in a small book, *Fifty-two Weekends out of Paris*. Never a disappointment. Trips to the country, the many chateaux, gardens and the comfort of being able to view a restaurant or café's menu on the outside before entering was so useful, especially when, as we were, travelling with young children.

Together with a Foreign Affairs colleague, we shared a cottage located 120 km south of Paris. Mémillon, near Châteaudun – originally an orangerie of a nearby aristocrat's home converted to a weekender – was the ideal place to relax. Forest around, masses of bluebells in spring and an abundant variety of wildlife. Many a happy day was spent at Mémillon.

With an extensive network of autoroutes one could reach the south (Nice, Cannes, Monaco, Marseilles, to mention a few) and northern Italy to the east with equally easy access.

Two particularly interesting visits were to Carcassonne Castle in the south – the site of fierce religious wars – and le Baux in the southwest, where the mineral that we know as bauxite was first discovered. Anyone with an interest in the metal aluminium should visit le Baux.

Probably the most moving experience, which was repeated each of the years we lived in France, was a visit to Ypres to the north. Villers-Bretonneux, Fromelles and the Somme were never-to-be-forgotten scenes of some of the greatest losses of life of Australian soldiers in World War One.

On Anzac Day special services are held, and these received wide publicity in Australia. Not forgotten subsequently, but out of the news once the presence on this occasion, wherever held, of the Prime Minister and/or Governor General and Chiefs of Staff is no longer news. However, under the Gate in the main street of Ypres (smaller but very similar to the Arc de Triomphe in Paris), each and every evening since 1928 the 'Last Post' has been sounded in respect and memory of those Australians and other Allies who died. An astonishing expression of respect handed down through the families living there. One could physically feel the gratitude. Even when buying a film and wishing to pay, the shopkeeper said, 'No charge today, sir, for an Australian!'

A lovely lady, one Elsie Atkin who worked in the trade section of the Embassy, had a special connection. Her Australian father, who served in the war, married a French lady and stayed on in France. He spent almost all of his life as the representative of the Australian War Graves Commission caring for the many, many sites where deceased Aussie boys had been laid to rest.

Elsie never married, spent every annual holiday in Switzerland and had an encyclopaedic memory for train and airline timetables for journeys within France. Not necessarily very useful in the internet era, but nevertheless pretty impressive. We exchanged Christmas greetings with Elsie for thirty years, each year hers to us being a four-page handwritten letter detailing what she had been up to during the year. Elsie has now passed away.

Just two visits to Madrid, Spain, during the first year of posting proved a contrasting experience to France. Particularly the business hours of the Spanish: starting early and a siesta following lunch before returning to the office. Evenings began late with the third meal of the day seldom being taken before 10 pm. Memorable occasions were visiting the Prado Museum – just wonderful paintings. Though not really anxious to, I also felt I should go to a bullfight at least once. Arriving from Paris on a Saturday I hadn't realised that to obtain a ticket was virtually impossible. While chatting up the concierge at the hotel, without much success, I felt a touch on the shoulder and on turning was confronted by one of the most beautiful and elegantly dressed women I had ever seen, wearing a sheath white dress, high heels and a large broad-brimmed white hat. Wow!

She had observed my efforts while waiting with a group on their way to that evening's series of fights. Guests expected from the USA were unable to join them because of flight delay and a spare ticket was there for the taking in the VIP area at no charge!

After a couple of drinks we set off and first stop was the Bull Museum attached to the stadium. Every display, including many taxidermist-prepared heads of a bull, was a tribute to the bull – how each had fought. Placards below each detailed their bravery when facing picadors, matadors and all others responsible for antagonising them, until, with shoulder muscles bleeding from countless dart-like arrows thrust into that area to weaken it, the bull would drop its head, enabling the ballet-like, dancing matador to give the final sword thrust through to the heart. Brave yes, both bull and matador, but disgusting for an animal lover – especially as the bull never really has a chance.

However, here's the museum that is dedicated to the bull! Fascinating to read an inscription that praises a particular bull for the number of helpers gored or thrown over the fence, and particularly if the said bull has killed a matador. He is as famous as Sir Donald Bradman!

Lladró porcelain caught my eye, given we had several pieces – now of significant value. Imitations are available, but none compare, especially as most have resorted to no longer depicting classic religious figures.

Visits to North Africa (Tunisia, Algeria and Morocco) were undertaken twice a year with my program on the ground being coordinated by an Australian Trade Correspondent, who in each case was a local businessman with the necessary connections and knowledge of local conditions. There were limited prospects for assisting exporters develop a market except in expertise and equipment required to carry out dry-land farming and for certain consumer products, particularly grains and dairy products.

One such opportunity existed in Algeria. To further Australian interests required travelling with Agricultural Department officials in Algeria to a destination some 400 km south of Algiers. After driving across almost continuous desert we came across the classic oasis with palm-fringed waterhole and irrigated pasture and olive groves. An area where Australian dry-land farming expertise had very real prospects. Stone-picking equipment, clover/rotation pastures, for example. Incredibly, beneath the sand existed a very large water table ready to be utilised, other than just popping to the surface now and again to create an oasis.

When it was time for lunch we were escorted by local officials and Bedouin tribesmen to the shade of an olive grove, there to find colourful carpets laid out on which were low tables groaning with various Arab delicacies. In the centre was a whole spit-roasted sheep and as guest of honour (wish I hadn't been!), I was invited to dig out, with my forefinger and thumb, the eyes, and consume after dipping in a bowl of yoghurt – which was more like sour cream than what we would consider yoghurt. As I was doing this (no way one could refuse), the Concorde on its flight path from Buenos Aires via Dakkar to Rome passed overhead, clearly visible from its vapour tail against a clear blue cloudless sky, together with the very audible sonic boom as it passed through the sound barrier. Perhaps it was only me that reflected at that moment, that on the ground, it was a biblical scene, above late twentieth century.

In Algiers I always stayed at the Hotel St George. Situated on a steep rise amid beautiful gardens of palm and flowering shrubs, it was a sad day when it closed its doors in 1977. However, before then I was lucky to enjoy a welcoming atmosphere. On one occasion my room was that used by General Dwight Eisenhower, later to become President of the United States of America, but then Chief of US forces in North Africa during World War Two. A well, and daily, polished plaque on the door a constant reminder that this had been Ike's room. I doubt however that the bed was the same.

I only had dinner on my own on the rare occasion, usually being out with representatives of companies that were agents of an Australian company, or a prospect to be so, accompanied by Bob Turner, Australia's Trade Correspondent to Algeria. However, when I did, I usually ordered half a bottle of Algerian red wine, at that time not very good, until one evening the waiter returned with a full 750 mL bottle of what he thought I might like to try. He had no idea what it was like, but many cases were found during renovations that necessitated the knocking down of a cellar wall. No less than Châteauneuf-du-Pape vintage 1939 from the south of France. On enquiring of the price the response was, 'No idea, sir, but less than the local wine as it can't possibly be as good!'

I bought five cases and onsold them to Bob who subsequently purchased several more cases for a song. Unfortunately, I couldn't take them back to Paris on the plane.

Morocco being a Royal Kingdom was in many ways a completely different experience. Slowly changing, but then Moroccans generally paid unswerving homage and loyalty to the King. Whilst Casablanca and Tangier were the commercial centres, the capital was situated in Rabat, somewhat detached from the real world. In many ways a bit like Canberra is to the rest of Australia!

Unfortunately I never had the opportunity of travelling extensively to centres such as Marrakech, but one very interesting visit was to the large tomato-producing farm of the Heinz-Sagima Company. Situated some 130 km north of Casablanca out of the small town of Kenitra, it was managed by George Fuller, an Australian. Harvesting was in full swing, all picking by hand by dozens of colourfully dressed Moroccan women bent over to the task. It seemed that all one saw disappearing over the horizon was the backside of these usually young ladies!

These bright red tomatoes were loaded into carts, brought into the main factory and tipped into water tanks to remove unwanted soil etc. An auger then directed them to a series of autoclaves, the steam in which removed skins, after which they were pureed and packed into 44-gallon drums for shipment to Heinz factories around the world, principally Europe, for the production of the many tomato-based products that have the familiar Heinz brand. Of interest was that these tomatoes, though red and ripe when picked, could be bounced like a tennis ball. Inedible in a salad, specially bred so that they could be handled without the skins splitting when moved from field to being pulped.

In Tangier I experienced something for which I had not been prepared by training or natural instinct – the judging of a teenage belly dancing competition! Put up to this by a lovely couple, Wynand and Lorna Goyart, he being Dutch-Australian, she Australian. They lived in Tangier where Wynand was CEO of a firm producing very high quality menswear in the Export Processing Zone. The Goyarts' daughter Belinda was a contestant. She didn't win, but it turned out to be a hilarious evening, one during which I secured my belly dancing judging wings!

Our time in France will be most remembered by a special date, 23 June 1977, the day Benjamin David came into the world to join Anne-Marie and Marc, and very special, given the loss of David in Bangkok. His arrival completed a family with which we are blessed, international by any criteria – at least by that of birth.

John, father, born in Malaysia
Maureen, mother, born in Canberra
David in Hong Kong
Anne-Marie in Taipei
Marc in Bangkok
Benjamin in Paris

A situation that caused much interest on the part of migration officials when entering Australia on our many return journeys between postings.

In the very week we were due to leave Paris for our next assignment, that of Jakarta, Indonesia, with five years of unforgettable experiences, those described being only a few of the many, we had one that we could well have done without.

Very heavy rain over a weekend in mid June threatened flooding of the Seine. It was the Sunday afternoon and suddenly we were without power, some eight levels up. I rang the building's security office and was met with a voice that clearly expressed concern, even a measure of panic. The level of the Seine had backed up into the stormwater pipes that carried flood waters from the whole Embassy complex roofs into the river. The pipes burst resulting in the flooding of three levels of underground car parking, inundating the squash court, swimming pool and 'electrics room'. For three hours a few of us pushed as many cars as we could out into the street (many owners away for the weekend or just out and about in the city). I literally collapsed on the bed, completely exhausted as never experienced before.

But our troubles had only just begun, because although we moved out into a hotel as power wasn't to be restored for several days, the packers were due on the following day. Every piece of packing material had to be walked up eight floors and every box carried down. No lifts working. Design fault? Ask Harry Seidler!

And so we finally took off from Charles de Gaulle Airport for home via New York, Los Angeles for a few days in Disneyland, and then on to Sydney.

A challenging posting and one that before undertaking I would strongly advise any appointee to take French lessons and read at least the following:

- *Sixty Million Frenchmen Can't Be Wrong* by Jean-Benoit Nadeau, and certainly;
- *A Family in Paris – Stories of food, life and adventure* by Jane Paech

A must for anyone moving to live in Paris making a home in a strange land and finding a community.

By way of a personal postscript, a much remembered and cherished account of our first Christmas, which was spent in Norway.

A Norwegian shipping company representative, Anders Andersen, and his family became close when we were stationed in Bangkok, strengthened by the friendship of their son, also Anders, and our David. Both families were transferred from Bangkok at about the same time, we to Paris, they back home to Norway, to their hometown of Tonsberg, situated south of Oslo on the Oslo Fjord between Drammen and Sandefjord. Anders's father had been a harpooner in the Norwegian whaling fleet and he spent his early years at school in Perth, Western Australia, and some holidays accompanying his father on hunting forays out of Albany. Home base for the fleet in Norway was Sandefjord, subsequently the retirement home of young Anders's grandfather. Gateways to the town of the jaw bones of whales made it very evident as to the historical reason for the existence of Sandefjord.

We had lost our David before proceeding to Paris so an invitation to spend our first Christmas with the Andersen family (yes Anders Andersen II father, Anders Anderssen III David's friend) was very special. Our journey by car took us to overnight in Hamburg from Paris and then by overnight car ferry to Oslo and thence the drive down the coast to Tonsberg. Snow covered the ground and darkness fell soon after three in the afternoon. Early evening saw small elf-like faces at the windows. It was explained that these were some of Santa's helpers checking as to who the extra children were that had to be included in Santa's present drop. This was the night of 23 December. Soon as darkness fell on Christmas Eve, children all over Norway, accompanied by their fathers, went to their local church for a happy hour of hymn and carol singing (no service), during which the young ones were allowed to roam all over the place happily chattering, singing and laughing.

When the time came to leave, at the same time countrywide, one exited to an incredible cacophony of sound as virtually every church bell in the whole land was rung. The combined sound of bell chimes echoing over valleys and mountains was nothing short of thrilling.

Prior to leaving the house the children had placed porridge and carrots at the front door for Santa's reindeers when he called for his present drop! On returning, dishes were checked – all empty – and presents were arranged around the tree.

Then the door bell rang! Who could be there? A rush to open the door and disbelief on the faces of the young was a memory that will last forever. There was Santa with a reindeer! He had forgotten to leave a parcel! Santa bid farewell and the door was closed. All of these events (faces at the windows, Santa's return) had been set up by Anders's family with the help of village friends just for these welcome strangers from Australia!

Magic, never to be forgotten.

CHAPTER SEVEN

Jakarta, Indonesia

1979–1983

At the time of taking up my assignment, I believed Indonesia was the most important country with which Australia should be developing relations. A much belated increase in focus on Asia generally has taken place towards the latter part of the past thirty years, mainly on China, but increasingly including India and rightly and realistically so. Indonesia however, is our closest neighbour, a Muslim country, having a population in excess of 200 million and largely not understood by most Australians. If questioned about what they knew about Indonesia, the average person confronted in the street would hesitate and then say, 'Oh, yes, Bali.'

Prior to engaging with Indonesia, in whatever activity, it is necessary to quickly come to understand the many complexities of Indonesian beliefs and character, which have flourished after Independence in 1949–1950 under President Soekarno. Independence was actually declared on 17 August 1945 at the conclusion of World War Two in the Pacific.

Indonesia is a very complex nation with its inhabitants spread over 13,000 islands, speaking many different languages/dialects. Whilst many dialects still exist, Soekarno recognised the need, to ensure unification, for one official Indonesian language. Cleverly he chose that of one of the least spoken. This eliminated the danger of exclusion/isolation and therefore disconnection of many parts of the country.

Indonesia has been compared with the experience one has when watching a fan dance. 'You think you get glimpses of it, but you never do!'

Officially the basic philosophy of the country, of the people, is governed by five fundamental principles, collectively, Pancasila.

- Belief in one supreme God,
- Humanity,
- Unity of Indonesia, bringing together over 300 ethnic groups and dialects,
- Democracy led by wisdom of deliberations among representatives,
- Social justice for all.

It is important to recognise that, particularly amongst the Javanese, there exists a strong dislike of disharmony. Traditionally issues are settled through:

- Musyawarah, a process of tedious consultation, this leading to:
- Mufakat, a consensus.

Business and culture – rarely will these two unlikely companions feel at ease together, but we, as the foreigners, MUST come to terms with the tensions that exist between the two, given that they lead to many important practical considerations. One example being that the initialling of an agreement often indicates that the Indonesian party has agreed that the document forms an acceptable basis for negotiation – nothing more. Remember I am recalling the period when I was working in Indonesia. Now some thirty years later customs/attitudes may have changed somewhat.

Overall the key is face-to-face relations, even though communications have changed so radically as a result of advances in modern technology. There exists a strong urge towards harmony. If by expressing the truth, displeasure will be inflicted, then truth will simply be withheld as it brings shame to the perpetrator. This can result in the saying 'Yes' but meaning 'No' syndrome, or saying what you think the other party would like to hear, which may not be the truth.

Reminds me of the diplomat/lady story. When a diplomat says:

Yes – means maybe
Maybe – means no
No – he/she is no diplomat

When a lady says:

No – means maybe
Maybe – means yes
Yes – she is no lady

Seriously, though – and here I would like to quote from a speech given at a meeting in Jakarta in the mid 70s by a senior government official:

> Conflicts in words and conflicts in feeling should be avoided, even at great personal and psychological cost. In conversations and negotiations with others all parties should try to emphasise the items everybody agrees with, whereas conflicting matters should not be discussed for fear of hurting the feelings of others. This type of relationship makes it almost inevitable that a clear and outright, 'NO' as an answer to some suggestion is taken as a crude and unrefined behaviour. If one wants to say, 'NO' the polite way to do it is to say, 'Yes, but …'. What comes after the word, 'but' really carries the negative message. More difficult to catch is the Javanese, 'No' formulated in the word, 'Yes', but denied by facial expression or behavioural rejection.
>
> In essence the Javanese … 'Yes' in most cases means, 'I do understand you', and is far from, 'I agree with you', and even farther from, 'I promise to do what you want me to do'.
>
> Recognising the subtle feelings of the Indonesian and particularly those of the Javanese, it is advisable NEVER to make him ashamed in the presence of others. In fact the feeling of shame is a function of degrading of respectability in the eyes of other people. There is never a feeling of shame with an individual who is entirely alone with no other human being to watch or hear him.

Complicated? Not really if one is prepared to listen and try to understand.

Notwithstanding the preceding, one must also recognise that bribery is endemic. It's a question of degree and one must leave room to negotiate. After all, in Australia, at Christmas, the salesperson of a company will take a gift (case of beer, bottle of Scotch, half a dozen wine) to the buyer of his main clients to say, 'Thank you for your business, which hopefully will continue to grow over the year ahead'. Not really very different. Just a question of degree.

Finally, before leaving the important matter of differing customs and psychologies, a story told to me by Mr Radius Prawiro, then Minister of Trade, later to become Governor of the Central Bank of Indonesia, which adds a dimension that a Westerner coming to live and work in Indonesia would previously have been totally unaware.

The setting is in Solo (Java), the women of this area being central in the handling of the family finances and having a reputation for being just a little cunning. Under the shade of a large tree sits a fan seller. She has one basket with fans being offered for 500 rupee each, the other contains very similar looking fans for 5000 rupee each. A potential buyer stops, handles one of each, then decides to buy one of the cheaper fans. Money exchanges hands, and whilst walking away, the unsuspecting individual opens his newly acquired purchase and fans his hot sweaty face. In a short time, the fans falls to pieces, which results in a quick return to the seller, accompanied, on arrival, with a heatedly delivered complaint. Without a smile on her face, the explanation is given.

'Oh, the 5000-rupee fan you open, hold in one hand, and wave back and forth to create cool air. With the 500-rupee fan, you open, hold in one hand and move your head from side to side to create a breeze!'

Arrival in a city, a country, in Jakarta, Indonesia, presented us with a very different environment from Paris, France. Postings in Asia, particularly that of Bangkok, provided a good background to the stresses and strains that a posting in a tropical climate would face a family with three young children.

After a few days at the Borobudur Hotel we moved into a home complete with a clutch of servants, inherited from our predecessors. Without going into detail, these conditions proved totally unsatisfactory, so a move to the other side of the city was made. Some interesting early experiences awaited us. One such item, was that the towel rails in the main bathroom were 'alive'. Attachment screws into the wall were in contact with live wires running along the timber frame behind. Subsequently we also discovered that several village homes over the boundary fence were drawing their supply from us! A not uncommon occurrence in Indonesia. They received quite a shock when their lights and TVs were suddenly no longer functional.

We enrolled Marc and Anne-Marie in the Jakarta International School (JIS), a school with a 2000-plus student body, ten per cent of whom were Australian. The program was based on the US system of education, which proved excellent and complementary to the French system previously experienced. The latter was strict, no parental involvement, which taught the children how to learn. Interestingly there was a strong emphasis on reading and eventually composing poetry. At the JIS freedom of expression was encouraged from an early age. Confidence-building activities were important in the classroom and on the field. The involvement of parents was not only encouraged, but mandatory, especially with sporting programs, where guided by a few experienced coaches, all sports competitions only existed because of the participation of parents.

Overall our experience with the 'International School' system overseas was very positive, at least up to the level of Year Eight (age eleven to twelve), when we believed our children should complete their secondary schooling in Australia if they were to develop an Australian identity – with country and making of lifelong friends during those formative years into their late teens. So regardless of where we were, they were at boarding school in Adelaide and all flourished. We couldn't be prouder parents.

An unexpected turn of events occurred when I was asked if I would join the board of the JIS. Very time consuming, but so worthwhile, as I was able to represent the families of the 200 or so Aussie students. Board responsibilities took on another dimension when almost half the school, which was a great campus, burnt down. Many late into the night board meetings were necessary as a consequence.

One major new experience was that of being introduced to, and having to listen to, the wishes, concerns and indeed demands, of members of the Parent Teacher's Association, the PTA. I weathered the storm, but once in a lifetime was enough!

Issues and opportunities for Australian companies covered a broader spectrum than those at any of our other postings. In assisting newcomers to the complexities of doing business in Indonesia, one could draw on the experiences of many already well established in the market, as well as those which had not been successful. Australian companies were/are involved in mining, manufacturing, service industries (legal, accounting, architecture et al.), fishing, building materials (concrete), drilling (water, oil, gas), household products (Kiwi), asbestos sheeting, travel (Qantas), banking, education, industrial gases, aluminium extrusions, glass, packaging materials, fasteners (Ramset), and metal and pipe extrusions (Tubemakers), to list a few.

Visits of Australian businessmen and women were numerous, resulting in always full and active business hours and evenings of social events taking up an average of five nights a week. Opportunities to relax, either in the Puncak (the tea gardens in the hills), or on the coast at Carita, were welcome and necessary.

Situated at 1000 metres or more above sea level, in the Puncak the Embassy had a number of houses available for staff where they and their families, on a rostered basis, could enjoy a most welcome break from the sultry heat of Jakarta. The modest elevation ensured cool mornings and nights, with walks and horse rides through the green lush tea gardens being very beneficial. Carita, situated on the western end of Java, overlooked the Sunda Straits and the ever active Krakatoa volcano a few kilometres across the sea towards Sumatera. Weekends in a simple cottage right on the beach were magic. Wonderful swimming, unbelievable sunsets and daily visits by fishermen offering a range from their overnight catch. Lunch coupled with a cold beer or midday gin and tonic, made returning to Jakarta on a Sunday evening an unwelcome event. Whilst most business decisions, certainly where the government was the authority, were made in Jakarta, there were sound reasons to venture into the provinces during one's posting, especially to Surabaya, where Austrade maintained a sub-office, but also to Jogjakarta, Cilacap and Bandung, all located on the island of Java.

Sumatera (Sumatra), its people and geography noticeably different from that of Java, was the location for Caltex's main operations, the largest of all foreign investors in Indonesia, and that of PT Indonesia Asahan Aluminium, an integrated hydro station and aluminium plant, and a Japanese joint venture. On a leisure note, no one should visit Sumatera without visiting Lake Toba, a large elevated lake to the north. A popular holiday resort, with good reason.

The island of Batan was developing into an area of special interest, with the planning of an export processing zone and for tourism. Situated closer to Singapore than Sumatera, Batan has become an item of interest for tourists visiting Singapore, being a relatively short journey by ferry from Singapore.

The Australian Ambassador to Indonesia, in order to visit otherwise not easily accessible areas of Indonesia, had access to a STOL aircraft, operated by the RAAF at Butterworth, Malaysia. Pilots were required to clock up a minimum number of flying hours on these C-130s and providing this facility met both needs. On one such visit to Sulawesi, Maureen and I accompanied the Ambassador, his wife, and a team of civilian and defence officials stationed at the Embassy. A memorable week-long visit to a very interesting and different part of the world.

The highlight was a weekend stay at the guest facilities of PT International Nickel on the shores of a large lake at Soroako, Ujung Pandang. The lake – probably of volcanic origin – is the second deepest lake in the world after a lake in eastern Russia. The water so pure one can drink untreated, as well as having negligible surface tension. An outbound motor propelling a boat at a significant speed left virtually no wash in its wake. Apart from the usual club facilities in a major mining location, the highlight for recreation were the pontoons fitted with sun canopy, barbecues, ice-boxes and seating that were used as a platform for a day on the lake, lunch and swimming.

We shall long remember the hospitality of Jim and Barb Gairy, President Director, Ross and Judy Chapman, John Gill and Dr Usman Elfendi, Superintendent of Public Affairs.

From Soroako we flew north to the western end of the long east–west arm of Sulawesi, overnighting in a mountainous area where eel farming was one of the main activities. Eels you might say, what's so special? Special indeed, in that these eels were as large as a small dolphin! We slept in rudimentary accommodation and awoke to a breakfast that had been prepared by staff before they retired the night before. A fried egg standing uncovered for several hours in a warm, humid climate is not very appetising!

From there on to Manado in the far north-west. Here there are many special customs, one of which drew our particular attention – that of burying their dead in a sitting position. This required graves a bit deeper, but many more could be included in any given area. We also visited the area of Toraja, where doll-size images of one who had died (carved, coloured – the full bit), were placed in cavities cut into the cliff in full view for all to see. Colourful and very lifelike.

With local dignitaries combining to make up a large party, we were to be taken to outer islands north of Manado to view the making of wooden fishing boats using century-old techniques and also colourful coral reefs that were being considered as a tourist attraction waiting to be developed. As the boat we were in moved away from the wharf into mid harbour, a large water spout appeared in the hull showering all aboard, whilst we slowly sank! One member of the crew was instructed to plug the hole with toe, finger, whatever, whilst a relief vessel pulled up alongside, to which we transferred, and disembarked where we had started some half an hour before, never getting out to our original destination. All of this in full view of a large crowd doubled up laughing at the problems being experienced by a bunch of foreigners and local officials.

On our way home to Jakarta a stopover was made in Makasar to experience a meal at the Surya Restaurant, famous for its crabs. A several storeyed concrete building, stairs from the main tabled area led upstairs. We soon observed that crawling down the stairs from the floors above were an army of crabs! Turned out that baskets of these agile creatures were kept on the flat roof and many had escaped and presumably could hear the sound and smells of the sea and were heading home! Much amusement as staff scurried around trying to recapture these critters!

Our overall lasting impression of visits to various areas of Indonesia was the variation in housing construction and woven fabrics. In their traditional dress one came to recognise where an individual came from. All in sharp contrast to what one experiences in Australia, at least on a day-to-day basis.

Stories from our time in Indonesia are many, but two of particular interest warrant relating.

Planning his visit to Melbourne to attend an Indonesian Trade Display, the Minister of Trade, Radius Prawiro, asked me if I would accompany him and the large contingent of officials and businessmen that would be going. Obviously, my response was, 'Yes, of course.' There was one proviso, this being that we fly Garuda one way and Qantas the other. Fair enough.

Whilst in Australia the Minister expressed a wish to visit a sheep station and also a supplier of goods and services to the wool-growing industry. With the assistance of the Department of Foreign Affairs and Trade (DFAT) and our Melbourne office, these requests were readily met. First, over a weekend we were guests at a property that had come to specialise in welcoming VIPs such as Radius, including a delightful lunch before which the Minister was treated to a shearing demonstration, the classing of the fleece, and finally the castration and tailing of male lambs. To carry out the latter, each lamb was placed upside down in a cradle and quicker than the eye could follow, both procedures were completed, culminating in the lambs testicles being flicked into the air over the operator's shoulder, then immediately consumed by one of the several waiting dogs! The Minister was aghast, not at the operative's skill and speed, but at the waste of the testicles! He suggested that these should be collected, frozen into blocks and exported to Indonesia, where animal testicles, particularly those of bovine origin are a delicacy. Why not sheep's? Incidentally, each evening in a particular area of Jakarta, a row of street stalls opens offering nothing but grilled or boiled male animal private parts. As far as I know the Minister's suggestion was never followed up!

A visit to the showroom of Goldsbrough Mort took place early in the week following the sheep station visit. At the Minister's shoulder I followed him around, he showing great interest in every item on display that had any relevance to the raising of sheep, from shearing machinery to sheep dips and a multitude of items between. An aide with a pad and pen was close by, and it became evident that the Minister wished to order, for shipment to his farm in the hills outside Jakarta, one of everything. Whilst this process was continuing a member of the office staff asked me who was the buyer and could I explain why this very unusual order was mounting and how big was the Minister's property, how many sheep, etc. etc.? When I reported that he had probably not more than two or three sheep, there were gasps of amazement and controlled mirth. Anyway, everything was packed up and accompanied the Minister back to Jakarta on Garuda Airlines.

Some weeks later I received a photograph from Radius, dressed in farmer's clothes, standing next to a sheep that he had personally shorn using the one stand unit purchased with an accompanying note expressing satisfaction with himself, in that it had taken him two days to complete the task!

Prospects of developing a wool industry in Indonesia were always doomed, given the tropical climate (heat and humidity) would cause great distress and the almost certainty of many conditions, such as foot rot, being endemic to the proposed industry.

At the time of my posting the Northern Territory Government, under the leadership of Paul Everingham, developed a close relationship with Indonesia – particularly as there were very good prospects for the development of live cattle exports and also an interest in attracting Indonesian investment into the Territory. President Suharto had a mixed farming operation in the hills outside Jakarta devoted to upgrading the breeding stock of a wide range of animals, which would be distributed to rural areas. The aim was to develop cattle that produced more milk and meat, chickens that produced more meat and eggs, etc.

The NT Government offered to present President Suharto with the prize-winning Zebu-Santa Gertrudis bull at the Katherine show. The offer was accepted. Then came the planning for delivery, which included ensuring the obtaining of maximum publicity.

The big day came, a Saturday morning, on the runway at Jakarta International Airport. There gathered a group of Indonesian Department of Agriculture and Australian Embassy officials, including yours truly. On schedule the RAAF C-130 aircraft landed, taxied to a halt, and the rear loading bay door dropped. A large beautifully and specially made crate was rolled out with the massive prize winner inside. This was loaded onto a waiting truck for immediate transportation to the President's farm. Ceremony was minimal.

The following day we journeyed to the hills, accepting the President's invitation for a barbecue (no, not the bull!), and for Paul Everingham to preside over the official handover of this handsome gift. This took place accompanied by the pedigree placed in a hand-carved wooden folder and a large sash of NT colours. A relaxed day followed, which included a tour of the farm in a fleet of army vehicles and a large contingent of heavily armed military to deter any assassination attempt.

Several months later I received a call from the President's office, expressing the President's disappointment that the prize bull was not earning his keep, in that to date he had refused to service a single

Indonesian female of the species and, as far as I know, certainly up until the time that I left Jakarta, that remained the situation. One presumes that in the final event he tasted good!

And so the time came to move on, to a very different assignment, to Seoul, Republic of Korea. As a family we enjoyed living and working amongst friendly and generous people and increasingly recognising the growing importance of Indonesia, our nearest neighbour.

The decision to move was made for us, but had this not been the case and we stayed on for a few years more, we may have ultimately had to consider the following:

You know you've been in Indonesia too long when you:

- find yourself accepting as logical that the houseboy needs the week off and a 25,000 rupee loan for the fourth death of his uncle
- tell the cook to put more peppers in the *nasi* (rice)
- start carrying all your luggage on the plane with you
- look forward to a dinner of local steak
- don't even flinch when your driver cuts across four lanes of traffic and zooms between two speeding buses
- begin to enjoy cold showers
- discover that the footprints on the toilet seat are your own (my favourite)
- don't try to peer under the blacked out spaces in *Newsweek*
- eat durian and love it
- look forward to a relaxing drive to Puncak or Anyer
- start putting $10 notes in your passport at customs in Sydney
- do everything with your right hand except pick your nose and you are left handed
- only have diarrhoea once a month
- do your baking without bothering to sift the worms and bugs out of the flour.

If any four of the above have happened to you lately it's strongly recommended that you request a transfer.

CHAPTER EIGHT

Seoul, South Korea

1983–1987

From Jakarta to Seoul – what a change! A climate colder in winter and almost hotter in summer than we had ever experienced. A proud, hard, self-centred people and no wonder given their unique history – particularly from the late 19th to mid 20th century, when subjected to a harsh Japanese occupation from 1895–1945; fifty years, during which the teaching of the Korean language was prohibited, as well as the celebration of Korean festivals, even dress.

Our impression was that Koreans hated the Japanese. This 'national attitude' was largely fostered by President Syngman Rhee, though he kept the Japanese systems. As the Japanese had their large conglomerates (Mitsubishi, Toyota, Mitsui and their trading arms, Mitsubushi Shoji, Mitsui Shoji etc.), so Korea saw the establishment and rise of Samsung, Pohang Iron and Steel, Daewoo, Hyundai, Korea Heavy Industries, Kukje-ICC, Halla, Lucky-Goldstar International, etc. Employment with such '*chaebols*' was often/usually a 'cradle to the grave' commitment. Many have their own accommodation for employees, schools, hospitals and sports teams, together with stadiums.

After a short period of reconstruction following the end of World War Two in 1945, the country was again thrust into turmoil with the commencement of the Korean War, which lasted from 1950–1953.

Faced with starting all over again against the background of there being only a truce between North and South Korea – no peace treaty has been signed to this day – South Korea faced massive reconstruction costs, especially transportation needs, roads and rail in particular. Access to the port of Pusan on the east coast of the peninsula from Seoul was critical to the process. The port of Incheon on the west coast, and much closer than Pusan to Seoul, was not an option for shipping, as Incheon has a tide variation of over thirty feet, Pusan less than a foot. General MacArthur was acutely aware of this when leading a massive UN landing behind the North Korean-Chinese lines during the war. Had he mistimed the operation all vessels would have been stranded well away from the coast. An easy target to onshore North Korean batteries.

Korea applied to the World Bank for funds to build the Seoul-Pusan highway, a request that was turned down. Not to be denied, the Koreans built it themselves – largely with military labour.

As to social customs and structures, we soon realised that whilst an outwardly male-dominated society, women were very much in charge behind the scenes – particularly at the domestic level. The weekly pay packet was routinely handed over to one's wife, who then controlled the family's expenditure. Ewha Womans University's administration and student body consisted entirely of women, an interesting first for us. The mother to mother-in-law connection is strong as is the care of the elderly. In our period in Korea there were no old people's homes. All requiring care were attended to by the family.

There exists a preoccupation with the importance of education. More robotic than would be tolerated in our society, but it produced the engineers, doctors (often with little by way of bedside manners!), accountants, teachers that were required.

During my posting the daughter of the Senior Marketing Officer in Austrade's office was in her final year before entrance to university, culminating in a very competitive exam. She would come home from school, have dinner and immediately settle down to study. If/when requested, her mother would provide something to drink, but most importantly her daughter knew she was there, in the next room. Her father on arriving home would have dinner and go straight to bed. Around 9 or 10 pm he would take over 'duties' from his wife. Both father and daughter would go to bed around 2 am! This would be normal for six days a week for at least six weeks before exams.

Korean Patterns by Paul S. Crane, first published by Kwangjin Publishing Company for the Korean branch of the Royal Asiatic Society, fourth edition 1978, is still relevant when trying to reach an understanding of the Korean psyche. Required reading before taking up a posting in Korea, whether in the public or private sector.

Paul Crane was the son of missionary parents, a graduate of Johns Hopkins University having previously attended Pyongyang Foreign School prior to World War Two. A surgeon, then Director of the Presbyterian Medical Centre, Chonju. A major in the US Medical Corps for two years during the Korean War followed. He was recalled in 1961 to act as the official interpreter for President Kennedy, and then President Johnson, during visits to the US by Korean President Park Chung Hee and then for Johnson's state visit to South Korea in 1966.

The above detail is provided to support the credibility of Paul Crane. Getting to understand the people of Korea was the most demanding of all our postings. Just one example given by Paul, and confirmed by our experience, was that foreigners are/were regarded as 'unpersons', in the same category as beggars, prostitutes, criminals and, surprisingly, butchers! If I was addressed as a bastard, technically or simply because of a character flaw, I could deal with such an attitude, but an 'unperson' suggests that one doesn't exist and that is isolation in the extreme.

Business was dominated by the already referred to major conglomerates, the *chaebols* – their structure mirroring that of Japanese companies. They were multifaceted in their interests, and the employer/employee relationship was one providing not only lifelong employment, but also that of providing almost all of life's needs. Accommodation for single employees, education from preschool to university entrance, sporting facilities including company teams. Employees know exactly their place in the pecking order of authority. At every level he, seldom she, was answerable to whoever was their immediate boss, whose authority was never circumnavigated.

This meant one needed to establish at what level any issue was decided upon. One could waste a lot of time directing an Australian business person to someone who couldn't make the decision sought, but who would never admit it!

Another aspect important in the negotiation process was that many, in fact most, important decisions were taken over a long lunch or dinner. This included top government-to-government negotiations. Often a press release and photo of participants would appear in the following day's press showing parties leaving a particular establishment in the early hours, and announcing that a particular deal had been concluded by the persons shown in the photo, often at ministerial level where large contracts were involved, such as the conclusion of a large iron ore or coal supply contract between one country and Korea.

On the domestic front, for a foreigner on a posting we very early on received an important lesson in entertaining. Where a dinner party for eight to ten in one's home is arguably the most personal form of entertaining in our society, our first attempt to do this in Korea proved a disaster. Careful preparation, which included consultation with Korean staff and our one and only domestic employee at home, all seemed fine, until our first guest arrived with uninvited relatives!

'So sorry, hope you don't mind, but cousin Kim and his wife arrived unexpectedly from Pusan.'

From then on we never invited Korean guests for a limited number sit-down dinner. Always a buffet or for cocktails, which are clearly more flexible functions when accommodating unexpected guests.

From the ongoing North/South Korean tensions that persisted all the time, the US military and business presence was dominant amongst other foreign countries. The US Yongsan base in the centre of Seoul was a city within a city. Access to its base hospital and club facilities made life much more comfortable for a foreigner carrying a diplomatic passport or a resident US citizen. The Sadan Pubin Seoul Club, with its many facilities, provided much required recreational facilities for expatriate members, especially those with young families. The Seoul Foreign School, which our son Ben attended, provided an excellent education prior to most students taking up their secondary education, (years eight to twelve) back in their home country.

We quickly learned to like and enjoy Korean cuisine, though this requires a taste for garlic. We shall never forget the atmosphere when confined to the lift of a high-rise! One either ends up loving or loathing kimchi, the cabbage-chilli-garlic combination traditionally put down in large ceramic jars for the winter months. Strong in flavour and rich in vitamin C!

It was in Seoul we acquired our beloved dog Sam, a Japanese dosa. This breed introduced to Korea during the period of Japanese occupation as a much feared guard dog – look at the photograph and make your own judgement – is a prohibited breed for entry into Australia, because of its reputation. Whilst gentle with the family and anyone who visited, provided they were suitably introduced, Sam was nevertheless very questioning of unaccompanied strangers, as we found out when living in Frankfurt, our next posting, where Sam joined us. More of that later.

A feature of the city of Seoul was the labyrinth of underground 'streets' and rail tunnels. The 'streets' originally constructed to provide shelter from air attacks for Seoul's significant population, were lined with shops and businesses. One could walk from one side of Seoul, north/south, east/west, and not come to the surface. The traffic at ground level was a sufficient reason to stay below.

Visits to the demilitarised zone between North and South Korea were frequent. Situated on the 38th parallel at Panmunjom are a group of buildings, some north, others south, of the parallel. The main room used for meetings of representatives from the North and South contains a long conference table down the middle of which the microphone cables ran – the official border between the two Koreas and simply a continuation of the fence outside separating the two countries. At one end are two small table flags, that of each State.

Originally, and lasting many months, a bitter dispute existed in that each of the Korea's insisted that their 'pole' was the taller. Each alternatively increased the height of theirs until the poles reached the ceiling! Finally, sense prevailed, and both are exactly the same height. When one looks across the border to Kaesong into North Korea one sees the tallest flag pole in the world with the largest national flag fluttering – that of North Korea.

This situation has existed at the ceasefire line since 27 June 1953. A truce to the war was never signed. In March 2013 North Korea unilaterally cancelled the ceasefire and officially re-established a state of war, a war that began in 1950, sixty-three years earlier.

We travelled extensively around Korea including the island of Jeju off the southern coast, but the most interesting weekends away were those arranged by the Royal Asiatic Society that took one to locations far off the tourist paths. Walks through gorges to caves in which hermit monks lived, to ancient ruins of societies long gone, to modern locations such as that of the Won Bok Fishery Company, a trout and salmon hatchery and fishery that had as major customers the leading hotels and retail outlets in Seoul. We arranged to be included in the delivery schedule from time to time. Fresh live fish netted from a large tank on the back of a truck into a laundry tub, then requiring immediate killing, filleting, packing and freezing, provided a culinary treat for meals to come.

An event of some significance took place at the launching of the *Kowulka*, (an indigenous word meaning 'crow'), at the massive Hyundai shipyards in Pusan. In a jointly owned venture by CSR and SA Gypsum, the vessel, some 20,000 dwt, if my memory serves me correctly, was built to carry gypsum from South Australia to Queensland back loading with raw sugar to CSR's refinery in Sydney. The gypsum was used in the production of bagasse-based plasterboard in Queensland.

In liasing with Hyundai officials regarding some of the arrangements, one of their requests was that I would bring the bottle of champagne to be used by Lady Neale, wife of Sir Eric Neale, later to be appointed Governor of South Australia. Maureen and I drove to Pusan the day before the ceremony, carefully nursing, not one, but two bottles, just in case! Changing in our hotel room before dinner we thought that a pre-dinner tipple would be good and so disappeared one of the two bottles. Confident that one would suffice we slept soundly and handed over the one remaining bottle to Hyundai officials the next day, which turned out to be bitterly cold. Guests warmly clad in heavy jackets were assembled under a canvas awning on the wharf adjacent to the slipway to witness the event, which commenced with Lady Neale ascending the zigzag walkway ending at the platform facing the bow of the sparkling new *Kowulka*. Tied by the neck, the bottle of champagne, attached by a long cord was drawn back to the platform ready for, 'I name you *Kowulka* and may you and all who sail in you do so safely' etc., etc. The moment came, the band was playing and Lady Neale cast the bottle towards the bow. Alas, she wasn't wearing a glove, and the contents of the bottle were frozen, resulting in her hand sticking to the neck. No loss of skin, but contact of bottle and bow didn't occur, so the former had to be pulled back to the platform and launched again. No problem this time. A resounding smash and glass and frozen champagne sparkled in the sunlight as it fell to the ground. The moral of the story is twofold. First, don't leave yourself exposed by only having one bottle to play with, and second, if in a similar situation of officiating at such a ceremony in such conditions, always wear a glove!

Pre-luncheon drinks followed in the VIP guesthouse, an event attended by a large gathering of company executives, public servants and a scattering of diplomatic representatives including the Australian Ambassador, his wife and ourselves. I ventured to the men's room, a frequent necessity in such cold weather, to be joined by the most senior company representative from the Australian side. I finished, he remained. I washed my hands, he still remained, though noticeably having some problems with his clothing and being clearly agitated.

Offers of assistance were rejected and the said individual retired to one of the cubicles. He was wearing sheep's wool long-johns, ankle to neck to wrist, and he had them on back-to-front! I immediately realised what he had to do. Yes, completely undress and start again! I'm afraid I just collapsed in laughter and still had tears in my eyes when I rejoined the gathering. His wife was a little anxious, so when pressed, I explained the reason for the delay upon which all who were listening burst into peals of laughter, this scene being the one that he – I won't name him – faced when he re-entered the room.

Anne-Marie spent her gap year with us, keeping herself busy by running a pre-school for the young children of expatriates, at no charge, and for a brief period teaching English to young Samsung executives. Ben's time at the Seoul International School, already referred to, was a period he always remembers, because he was fortunate to have such a good teacher. He attributes his guidance in some measure to his future successes in life. Marc was at boarding school in Adelaide and, as did Anne-Marie, visited during school holidays. Lovely for us, as it was at all posts, and very educational for them.

Even thirty years ago, it was evident what a powerhouse South Korea would become. And so it has come to pass.

Once again it was time to move on, and one day, the call came from head office, 'What's your reaction to an assignment as Minister Commercial to the Federal Republic of Germany and Consul General based in Frankfurt?' The Australian Embassy was in Bonn.

As always, we only looked, as we could see it, on the upside of life awaiting us, and so we prepared for a second European posting. We arrived in Frankfurt in 1988, leaving Seoul just prior to the Seoul Olympic Games.

CHAPTER NINE

Frankfurt, Germany

1988–1991

Post included responsibilities for Australia's trade interests in FRG, Switzerland, Denmark, Sweden, Norway, Finland with responsibilities for sub posts in Hamburg, Copenhagen and Stockholm. Until late in 1990 sub posts in Berne and The Hague also reported to Frankfurt.

We had left Sam in Seoul whilst we returned to Australia for the usual spot of leave and briefing about my new post. Once settled in Frankfurt we gave Sam's carers the go-ahead to consign him on a direct Seoul-Frankfurt Lufthansa flight. With all the paper work in order, we entered the livestock/pet holding area at Frankfurt Airport and a call of his name drew an immediate loud barking response. When reunited the excitement was intense. The children were with us, on holidays from school in Adelaide, and Marc quickly took the lead as we made our way along a long corridor to where the final signature was given and Sam was 'free'. The very understanding gentleman in charge urged us to leave quickly for two reasons. The first was that in his excitement Sam could not stop wetting himself – he just peed and peed and peed! The second was that he had to urgently attend to the needs of several elephants that were transiting Frankfurt airport on their way to a European zoo or maybe zoos. This really put our situation into perspective!

Our first residence was out of the city on the edge of a forest close to the picturesque village of Friedrichsdorf. An early reminder of just what Sam meant to us and what his reaction would be to an uninvited visitor came one Saturday morning. Customarily, and this day was no exception, we would leave Sam outside when we went out.

The large garden was secure and the house locked. On this particular day we returned to find Sam barking at us from inside the house. A most distressing sight greeted the family on entering. The kitchen walls, benches and floor were covered in blood! Sam appeared a little shaken, covered in blood, but otherwise unharmed. The kitchen window was off its hinges and nothing seemed missing. Bravo Sam!

The police later explained that what had occurred was the action, in this instance unsuccessful, of a group that brought people from former Eastern bloc countries, gave them a home or homes to rob, took the goods, following which those that had entered the country by air would leave again the same day having received payment for their services. This made actually apprehending those responsible difficult.

On this particular occasion they were not prepared for the 'Sam Factor'! On entering through the kitchen window, Sam followed and clearly inflicted a severe wound on the arm or leg of one of those bent on carrying out the crime. Whilst carefully sponging Sam down we found no wounds other than a small abrasion, the result of a blow by a blunt object. All Sam needed was a significant dose of TLC.

The police said that they would send a 'dog whisperer' the next day, just to settle Sam, and for two or more hours we were treated to the delightful sight of 'cop and dog' together, the former talking away in German and Sam listening intently. We wonder even now how a German-speaking cop communicated with a Korean- and English-speaking canine! Anyway, at the time they seemed blissfully happy with each other's company.

Responsibilities associated with representation, (trade and consular) in a developed region contrasted with those in Asia. Those related to being Consul General, these being for the FRG only, were fairly minimal. The Australian Embassy located in Bonn assumed virtually all tasks of a diplomatic nature. Those related to the role of the Frankfurt Management Centre for Austrade were however very much widespread, (refer countries covered). A heavy tour program was necessary in support of the sub posts.

Participation, and support of individual exhibitions, in major trade displays dominated the post's activities. Mega trade displays such as CeBIT in Hannover, Automechanika in Frankfurt and the Book Show in Frankfurt were strongly supported by Australian companies, and required very significant assistance and servicing of individual needs by the post.

For me, characteristic German efficiency, preciseness and sense of order appealed greatly. I felt comfortable with their approach to life generally. That said however, there were several times when matters were taken to an extreme and one was reminded of Sgt Schultz, the humorous guard in the TV series *Hogan's Heroes*.

The first occasion came very early in our posting when invited to lunch at the home – I should say mini castle – of the Dean of the Consular Corps. We drove through large wrought-iron gates that opened automatically, parked where directed, were escorted through the front door and ascended a long stairway that curved to the upper floor. At several points on the way was located a pillar supporting a large birdcage in each of which was a brightly coloured macaw parrot! Guests were seated at a long, perfectly arranged table, some sixteen in all. The entree, *weisswurst* (white sausage), boiled and taken with a honey and mustard sauce was served by white-gloved waiters. Delicious and enjoyed by us on a regular basis today, they being readily obtainable in specialty supermarket stores.

However, try to picture the scene! I had no sooner cut into my sausage, as one does, when the hostess rose, placed herself behind me, then took the knife and fork from my hands and said, 'Herr Allgrove, you must learn how to peel the skin from the *weisswurst*.' With that she carefully slit the skin along the length of the sausage, deftly rolled it back using the fork and uttered a triumphant call, '*Voilà*, a properly prepared *weisswurst*!' Fifteen pairs of eyes fixed on me, and her, and indeed the sausage. Inwardly I was seething!

Other occasions included the well-dressed gentleman who admonished Maureen and I, ('bad example to the children'), for crossing a quiet suburban street when we should have done so at the traffic lights some 100 metres away.

One morning I awoke to a bloody nose that would not stop bleeding. After filling a not so small bowl, a towel with ice was applied and with the children, who again were with us on holidays, Maureen drove me to the local doctor. Where to park? The nearest space was part of a bus stop so urgent need required urgent measures. No sooner had we left the car than a first floor window opened and in not too dulcet tones, 'You are not permitted to park there. Move or I shall call the police.' I dropped the towel, faced the agitated individual and let him view a small torrent streaming from both nostrils. A quick retreat and the noise of a window being slammed shut! Some fifteen minutes later with nose having been cauterised and bleeding stopped, we returned home for breakfast.

One also had to come to grips with the German obsession for over engineering. Our first home contained a feature wall between the lounge and breakfast room that was an almost floor-to-ceiling fish tank some three metres high by almost a metre wide. A mass of water plants, dozens of fish, aerated and lit. It presented a most impressive sight. In the basement however, servicing this feature, was a veritable engine room of pipes, taps, filter beds and gauges that required constant attention if the fish were to survive. Needless to say we lost many.

Our second home had a non-functioning indoor swimming pool. Children used it for playing cricket and other ball games instead. The dormant plant that had been installed to keep the pool operational was on two levels, equal to the engine room of a small naval vessel. When one questions as to, 'why?' it became apparent that after World War Two it was a status symbol to have such plants to service, a swimming pool, laundry, heating/cooling system – even a fish tank.

Car manufacturers BMW, VW and especially Mercedes produced powerful heavy vehicles, built to go fast, and sit firmly on the road. Autobahns were constructed to cater for safe and high kilometre-per-hour speeds, so much so that the outer lane of, say, a six-lane (three each way) highway had no speed limit. Often travelling at 130 kilometres in the middle lane, one felt stationary as a Mercedes 300 flashed past at 180–200 kilometres per hour. One certainly heard the wrath of an agitated driver by way of a repeatedly pressed horn if they wished to pass and you didn't get out of the way.

A humorous, to us anyway, aspect of German autobahns was the sign indicating the next exit. It was AUSFAHRT! With situations such as exampled above one certainly was prone to '_ _ _FART'.

At the time of my posting in Frankfurt, the Australian navy was deciding what design of submarine should be chosen to replace its existing and well-worn underwater fleet. The need for a modern frigate was also under consideration. Areas patrolled and distances required to sail from home ports were important issues, not faced by many other developing countries. Does Australia choose a vessel 'off-the-shelf', or opt for a specially designed one. Dutch, American, Spanish, Swedish and German shipyards were contenders for both, or one, of these underwater and surface craft.

Several visits over a period of a couple of years to the Blohm and Voss AG shipyard in Hamburg, serious contenders for providing an off-the-shelf frigate and if my memory serves me correctly, also for the submarine. During this time I came to know well senior personnel, such as Dr Roh Kamm, Chairman and CEO of Blohm and Voss, and Peter Müller, ANZAC Project Management Coordinator in the FRG.

It was during one such visit that I was proudly conducted on a tour of the massive shipyard, with emphasis being given to the huge dry dock specially built for the construction of the *Bismarck*. In the hallway outside the Chairman's office was an impressive glass-cased model of the pride and joy of the German fleet from which special features were pointed out to me. In my position, diplomacy prevented me from saying what I was thinking almost out loud, 'Yes, very impressive, but where is the *Bismarck* now?' Quickly followed by, 'For that matter also, where is the *Graf Spee*?' For those too young to remember, both met watery graves early in the war.

The function of the post in countries such as Thailand, Hong Kong, Indonesia and indeed those surrounding the Mediterranean, was primarily that of servicing individual exporters and their agents. In Europe, however – other than very significant involvement in as already mentioned – major trade displays and meeting the varied requests of companies with on-the-ground offices was important. Victoria, WA, NT and Queensland all had Tourist Commission officers, Victoria also having a separate government office. Major banks as well as heavyweights, including CRA, TNT Express, Qantas, Western Mining, Australian Marine Engineering Consolidated (AMECON) and several others, had representative offices in Frankfurt or in one of the other major German cities.

Visits to Sweden, Norway, Finland, Holland and Switzerland were of a general servicing nature – Malmö in Sweden to visit Kockums Marine AB for issues associated with the submarine project being a significant requirement, but overall 'flying the flag' best describes one's activities during visits in support of the staff of sub posts in the region – particularly as locally engaged staff were so competent.

In 1990 the structure of Austrade changed. A largely private sector board was appointed, to which the occupant of the new position of managing director reported. A much flattened structure saw the creation of ten senior officers – Executive General Managers – each responsible for either an area of the world (six), or Australian-based functions (four).

Applications were invited for these ten Executive General Managers (EGMs), soon to be known as the G-10. I was successful in being selected EGM for South-East Asia, to be resident in Singapore, having responsibility for the management of Austrade's activities in this region.

In 1991 we moved to Singapore to take up this new position, which, whilst securing office space within the Australian High Commission, required purchasing suitable accommodation. In a country as well run as Singapore – government offices as well as the private sector – it was not long before we were settled in.

CHAPTER TEN

Singapore, Singapore

1991–1995

Post included responsibilities for Australia's trade interests in South-East Asia region included Singapore, Malaysia, Thailand, the Philippines, Indonesia, Brunei, Vietnam, Cambodia, Laos, and Myanmar.

My immediate responsibilities were spread over a large number of countries, half of which had a significant Austrade office with experienced staff on the ground for many years – namely in Singapore, Kuala Lumpur, Bangkok, Manila and Jakarta. My role was one of senior management – budget for the area, staff levels both Australian based and locally engaged, and given that Austrade as a whole had an expenditure ceiling, making the case to the board – through the Managing Director – of how much of the 'cake' should be spent in the region. Competition was very keen from EGMs putting their case for the countries for which they had responsibility. Regular travel, visiting posts within this region, was required. I have often referred to this final period of my career with Austrade, as spending 150 nights a year in one hotel room or another!

One constantly felt that Singapore itself was almost too good to be true. A benevolent dictatorship for a government ensured great stability and a society that worked. Government made it very clear to its citizens in the private sector – who were predominantly Chinese and Indian and naturally very entrepreneurial – that they should concentrate, in a very law abiding manner, with making money and let the government get on with the job of ensuring that they provided the environment to let them do so.

A society driven by meritocracy, in both the public and private sectors, saw, for example, the basic salary of the Prime Minister being that of the average received by the top professions in the private sector. At any one time these would have included those engaged in the banking, legal, medical and business sectors. The net result was, and I'm sure still is, that the PM of Singapore enjoys a basic income of several million dollars a year.

There is an oft quoted saying, 'If you pay peanuts to those running your country, you'll get monkeys filling the positions of greatest responsibility'. One has to make one's own judgment on this issue.

Most things worked in Singapore; Changi Airport a classic example. The ultimate benefits of the mandatory belonging to the Central Provident Fund another. Infrastructure always upgraded and efficient (for example road, water, electricity, telecommunications).

However, much came at a price to what we Australians would regard as being unacceptable – certainly politically. I have often thought, and still do, that a society somewhere between our form of democracy and Singapore's benevolent dictatorship would be ideal. Matters related to law and order for example. Issues becoming of increasing concern on our streets just don't happen in Singapore.

During our period in Singapore we witnessed, at various times, an approach to particular issues that would be unthinkable in Australia. Restricting the length of men's hair being one. An increase in the average weight of children being of concern saw measures that not only included dietary advice, through advertising and letters to the parents of affected children, but also – possibly as a last resort – that of humiliation in front of others in the classroom. Encouragement of the development of relationships between individuals having similarly high IQs, which might result in an increase in the number of gifted children in Singapore's society, was another.

Overall however, Singapore was a great place in which to live for the period we were there. Specialties such as chilli crab, drunken chicken and a host of other delicacies, went a long way to ensure this comfortable existence.

A most moving experience, almost as if it had to be, was being involved in events that took place over three days marking the fiftieth anniversary of the fall of Singapore on 15 February 1942.

Beginning late in the afternoon of Friday 14 February with a nurses service in St Andrew's Cathedral, there followed over the weekend a reception at the Australian High Commission, an International Commemoration Service at Kranji Cemetery where the Bastiaan plaque was unveiled, a ceremony at the Cenotaph arranged by the Chinese Chamber of Commerce and Industry, an 8th Australian Division Remembrance Service at Kranji Cemetary and other events held in Changi Gaol and the Changi Museum. Dr Ross Bastiaan set in place a plaque and time capsule ouside the main gates of Changi Gaol. A similar plaque was positioned at the Changi Gaol Museum.

Most memorable, however, were the evenings of poetry reading' arranged and hosted by Sir David Griffin CBE, formerly NX 69235 Sergeant Griffin D., who had spent the war as a prisoner in Changi Gaol.

I was asked by Sir David to be one of the three readers, with he being the moderator on each occasion. Also presenting were Col. Kerry Mellor, Australian Defence Attaché at the Australian High Commission, Singapore, and Tony Llewellyn-Jones, well-known actor and film producer who had spent many years in Singapore and Malaya. A background to this moving event follows.

How it all happened.

> In the first few weeks a far-sighted Australian, Brig. H.B. Taylor, anxious to maintain morale within the captured 8th Division, established the AIF Education Centre at Selarang. Staffed by soldiers experienced as lecturers and teachers it held classes in a wide variety of subjects from English literature to law and mathematics. Capt. Leslie Greener was its commanding officer and Sgt David Griffin one of its lecturers.
>
> In the early days men were invited to submit short stories, essays and poems to be judged by a panel – certificates being awarded to successful writers. From this the Changi Literary Society was born,

which continued to meet almost until the end of imprisonment. Its members were both Australian and British writers. The group met regularly to listen to original works submitted to it for criticism and constructive comment. As there was little or no paper – other than the back of prison forms – on which to write, all works were read aloud to the group either by the author himself or a nominated reader. Thus came into existence the collected poems written in Changi, a selection from which are to be read tonight.

The poems form a unique and deeply felt account of prison life as seen through the eyes of poets. A question is still often asked: What did it really feel like to be a prisoner with an indefinite or possibly life sentence? That question and a soldier's reaction to the total war experience has never been better answered than by the poems that are about to be presented. You will hear them exactly as they were written and you will be moved by them.

CHANGI DAYS

THE PRISONER AS POET

A selection of works by Australian and British poets for the Changi Literary Society 1942–1945

Selected and presented by
Sir David Griffin CBE
author of THE HAPPINESS BOX
formerly
NX 69235 Sergeant Griffin D.

A private contribution in remembrance of the Fall of Singapore

Selarang Camp 13 February 1992
Australian High Commission 14 February 1992
The Black Box
Fort Canning Centre 15 February 1992

Readers:

JOHN ALLGROVE

KERRY MELLOR

TONY LLEWELLYN-JONES

Special thanks:

THE AUSTRALIAN HIGH COMMISSIONER ALAN BROWN

COL SIN BOON WAH

COMMANDER, 9TH SINGAPORE DIVISION

BRETT MARTIN, FIRST SECRETARY (PUBLIC AFFAIRS)
AUSTRALIAN HIGH COMMISSION

THEATREWORKS (SINGAPORE) LTD

NATIONAL PARKS BOARD, SINGAPORE

NATIONAL INSTITUTE OF DRAMATIC ART, SYDNEY

DEPARTMENT OF VETERANS AFFAIRS, CANBERRA

AUSTRALIAN WAR MEMORIAL, CANBERRA

The program was made up of some twenty-six poems selected by Sir David from a much larger collection.

A practice session (only one), was held before presentation evenings, at which Sir David suggested which poems he and the three of us would read. He presented three of the collection that he had written himself.

Of the poems that I read, three in particular will stay with me forever. The first, as its background, has the campaign in Malaya with its wholesale slaughter of bewildered villagers by Japanese bombers. This prompted a protest, followed by a begrudging reconciliation in:

Night Bombing – Malay Village

Have you now messages, you palms that wait,
Locked in the silent night, knowing this hour?
Have you no warnings ere it is too late,
For these, the little people at your feet?

They planted you, sly palms, they gave you power,
Trusting in you for succour. Are you to fail
As sentinels of danger whispering near?
Your ears, not theirs, can catch the distant wail
Of night borne sirens, sick with fear.

Your children of kampong are asleep,
Brown, happy, innocent and unaware,
And Chinese tears are salty when they weep –
Have you no voice that they may hear?

Oh how loud your protestations yesterday,
When all the sky was filled with clouds and laughter,
Rustled your leaves then, swaying, singing,
Calling the naked Tamil boys to play!

Yet now the sky is filled – with what?
Darkness, two stars, and death, death winging,
And in the East the bright rim of the moon.
Traitorous palms, you hear and heed it not!

Come bombs, come death – come soon.

These children of the earth have never prayed
For more than life, some shadowy hereafter.
Wake not to learn that you have been betrayed,
Wake not to hear in horror, life's last word,
The parting call to Nothing, Hell or Heaven.
Stay silent palms, all is forgiven.

The sensitivity displayed by the author, in spite of his own desperate situation, is moving to the extreme.

The second, by an Australian, gives himself up to pure recollection of scenes from home. These are word pictures, but in the concluding lines he makes it plain that he has all but given up hope, 'and I have seen these things', he tells us, 'so what care I if there be no tomorrow to today'. The fight for the moment gone out of him.

Changi Meditation

I have known country mornings when the dawn
Cut patterns in the frost until it shrank
Into the hedge for shelter, and the wind
Nipped keen and crisp along the river bank
Skimming the wheat fields, whisking through the grass,
Ruffling the blear-eyed sheep who feebly bleat
Startled annoyance at the whirling hay,
And trot behind the stacks and stamp their feet.

I have known noisy bush days when the hills
Throbbed with the locusts gorgeously arrayed,
So that the basking lizard furls his frills
And flashes from his rock to seek the shade
Beneath the matted leaves of blood-red vines
Deep in a gully lit with bright moss flowers;
While from the steeples of the silver gums
The chimes of summer ring the passing hours.

I have known mountain afternoons,
With air so crystal still that you could hear
The plump of apples dropping to the earth,
The quiet water sliding from the weir,
The woody creak of harvest-laden carts,
The clink of harness and the straining trace,
The swearing of the drivers as they urge

Their blowing horses to their stumbling pace.

I have watched gum cities in the dusk,
Flicker with smoky lights of bushmen's fires,
Heavy with incense from the eucalypts.
On mountain ridges I have seen the spires
And pinnacles of castellated pines,
Jutting across the moon, old crumbling spars,
Buttressed by darkness, pinioned by the gloom,
Rising like grey cathedrals to the stars.

And I have seen these things, so what care I
If there be no tomorrow to today?
Remembrance lives, and beauty cannot die.

The third, a lovely example of how some managed to escape from the oppressive existence of being a POW. One such group were the poets. Let me here quote Sir David.

> With senses sharpened by a terrifying spiritual isolation the poet was able to steel himself to the agonies of composition. On its wings the poets in Changi were able to return to the days which many in their heart of hearts believed had gone for ever. It was a strange phenomenon that scenes and sensations which had apparently made little or no impression at the time suddenly sprang into focus in the poet's mind as though through the lens of an automatic camera. Thus a sparkling Australian day, an empty beach with great waves rolling towards distant headlands shrouded in their own mist, set the scene for the little drama in the next work.

The Excursion

Never, never will I forget, Uncle
That first sight of the sea.
The breathtaking sweep of it
The calm, the deep of it.
O the sea and the sound of the sea!

Where we had come from, Uncle,
Water was something in tanks.
Or yellowness lying in the river.
The river – did it run ever?
Save for the flow of red sunlight
Quivering between the sand banks
In the full flood of summer,
It ran never. No matter,
Nothing mattered in that withered township
With its iron roofs and pepper trees
Drooping in air
Aching with inarticulate despair!

Always, always I will remember, Uncle
That first shock of the waves.
The crumbling sugar white of them,
The din, the night of them
O the burst and spray of the waves!

Why did you bring me, Uncle,
A small boy prattleless with wonder?
Surely I was no companion
For this tremendous excursion.
Yet I hear you now,
Asking Aunt Polly timidly
Could you, could you take nipper
And show him water proper
With ships and all?

Ah, Aunt Polly
For all our feigned asperity
And non-conformist severity
How could you refuse him
Red-faced genial uncle?

For you, who hated the township
Which had burnt you, had scorched the sex,
The passion, the zest, all but the love
Out of you; This was goodbye.
And the little boy, the selfish, unkind
He saw the shadows in your eyes,
The inner eye of youth is seldom blind.

Uncle my first music was
The wet sound of the surf.
The slap on the shore of it.
The gasp, the snore of it.
O the rush and retreat of the surf!

We stood on this very spot, Uncle.
You – your braces; no tie
With your ruby stud doing duty
And I – I forgot, forgot all
Save the space and the blue and the beauty.
And those waves beating the sands were my waves,
And my breath was the salt wind
Skimming the spiny grasses.
While the voice, the voice
Of some primitive urgency
Swelled from my heart
Reared, curved, broke
On the rocks of me
O God – the sea!

And now you are dead Uncle,
And I am a mariner
With a frayed cap and kindly twinkle
As the children's mothers say.
And the township and Aunt Polly gone too.

But the waves and the wind
The white and the blue –
Oh Uncle;
Ruby stud and braces and all
You knew – you knew!

What a simply wonderful and tear-bringing expression of a young Australian country boy's memory of his first experience of the sea.

Of those countries which made up my region of responsibility, special mention should be made of Malaysia and Vietnam. Indonesia, so important to Australia, has already been covered, as has Thailand, having served postings there. Myanmar, a rich and interesting nation, I briefly experienced when on tour to Burma (as it was called then) from Calcutta. Restraints, for political reasons, between our two nations prevented me from touring Myanmar whilst in Singapore.

Under British colonial rule, the Malayan Public Service was staffed exclusively by residents of Malay descent, with only senior positions being filled by expatriates. Following independence, this policy was continued by the government, with positions previously being occupied by expatriates being made available to nationals of Malay descent only.

There was an oft repeated saying at the time, and indeed before, that if a Malay earned enough money to keep his family for two days, then he/she wouldn't present themselves for work on the second day. In the same situation, a Chinese would still show up for work the second day and invest the 'extra' money earned on the first.

Unrest between the two very different ethnic societies developed. One remembers the violent riots of 1968. In an attempt to arrest a Chinese 'takeover', several very unfair and racist measures were introduced. The percentage of Malays in the workplace was artificially maintained at a level in favour of Malay nationals. Entrance marks in order to enter a university for a Chinese were set higher than those required for Malays.

However, despite the preceding, and indeed the strains imposed during the Emergency (1948–1960), Malaysia has flourished, is stable and has been very successful in attracting significant foreign investment.

I greatly welcomed and enjoyed visiting Vietnam, these visits being made primarily to Hanoi and Ho Chi Minh City – still referred to by so many as Saigon. A resilient, hardworking people, the Vietnamese reminded me in many ways of our Korean experience. Tough colonial rule, the country split into two, a Communist north and a West-oriented south. The savage war of independence to forge one nation saw the unthinkable happen. The north triumphed over the combined forces of the south and the US and its allies. With remarkable energy, nationwide reconstruction and development has accelerated as each year following the end of the war passes.

Some 'habits' seemingly never die, or at least take several generations to change. Just two examples remind one of how important it is for an exporter to think laterally, to keep an open mind, and understand and accept that not everyone thinks and acts in the same way as we do here in Australia with our Western mindset.

The first was experiencing the frustration of an apple exporter (from NZ if I remember) who simply couldn't understand the constant disinterest he faced in trying to market his Granny Smiths. Many years of US-grown apples, filtered out of the PX during the war, had conditioned public preference to red apples with, and this was the second requirement, five points at the base. Grannies are green and don't have any points on the base.

The second, and with this I was involved in finding the solution, quite simple as it turned out to be. Gateway Pharmaceuticals knew that there was a demand for the various medications that they wished to market and that their prices were competitive. Why no interest? Finally it was realised that 'our way' of getting prescription medicines, or those freely available off the shelf, was by way of oral administration. Due to long years of French colonial rule a suppository was preferred!

In both cases politeness and avoiding loss of face on the part of the exporter, as seen by the Vietnamese, no explanation was initially given as to product rejection.

Incidentally, one experienced the reverse problem when stationed in Paris. Try getting your four-year-old son to accept a suppository shoved up his you-know-where, when an equivalent tablet swallowed with the help of a glass of water would have the same result!

A most pleasant reminder of previous French rule was that wherever one went in the country, each village passed through saw roadside stalls offering freshly-baked baguettes (bread sticks), alongside those selling the usual fruits, coconuts, coloured water drinks etc.

And so the time neared for me to 'hang up my spurs' as the saying goes, at least so far as a career in the Trade Commission Service was concerned. We did not look forward to leaving such a well-run nation. Its wonderful flower-filled airport, its equally brilliant botanic gardens – especially the orchid section – the zoo, particularly the enjoyment of having breakfast with the orangutans, and experiencing the tours by night when nocturnal animals and birds were up and about. The food, oh yes the food! And the energy of the people. All those are sadly missed.

We departed Singapore in September 1995, finally retiring from the service on my sixty-third birthday, 24 October 1995.

Epilogue

My chosen career would have been very difficult to undertake without the support of a close partner. The reality of responsibilities to be met were such that it was clear the government engaged the services and contributions of two, whilst only paying for one.

In my late teens and early twenties I was made aware that in order to lead a happy, successful life one had to address four important 'musts':

How fortunate was I in finding these 'musts', with the exception of that to be rich, in one woman!

- It is very important to find a woman who can cook and maintain a home.
- It is very important to find a woman who is rich.
- It is very important to find a woman who can endlessly keep you sexually satisfied.
- It is very, very important that these three women never meet!

However, as the years rolled by, the relative importance of these criteria changed. I found that it would help if I resorted to the ingesting of Viagra. The only problem was that the tablet got stuck in my throat, so that all I experienced was a stiff neck!

On a more general note, another prime requisite was that of appreciating and contributing to humour. It was easy to find sadness, even despair, but looking for a reason to laugh, to smile, was often a little more difficult. However, a smile, even open laughter – even though alone at the time – came from many and varied sources. Notices in English in non-English-speaking countries visited was one such source.

- In the elevator of a hotel in Paris: 'Please leave your values at the front desk.'
- In one's room in a Japanese hotel: 'You are invited to take advantage of the chamber maid.'
- On the faucet (tap) in a Finnish washroom: 'To stop drip, turn cock to the right.'
- At the desk of a hotel in Zurich, Switzerland: 'Because of the impropriety of entertaining guests of the opposite sex in the bedroom, it is suggested the lobby be used for this purpose.'
- At the bar in a Norwegian hotel: 'Ladies are requested not to have children in the bar.'
- In a Tokyo bar: 'Special cocktails for the ladies with nuts.'
- In the window of a Swedish furrier: 'Fur coats made for ladies from their own skins.'
- On the wall of a Bangkok temple: 'It is forbidden to enter a woman, even a foreigner, if dressed as a man.'
- And finally, in a Tokyo car rental brochure: 'When passenger of foot heave in sight, tootle the horn. Trumpet him melodiously at first, but if he still obstacles your passage, tootle him with vigour.'

Not exactly a humorous matter, but given the passage of time, it really is laughable today that previous opinions existed relevant to the employment of women Trade Commissioners fifty years ago.

I embarked on my first posting in Calcutta in 1962. Soon after I obtained a copy of an in-house minute paper dated 13 March 1963.

Today the glass ceiling, unfortunately, still exists – in some sectors more than others – but it would be unthinkable for anyone to originate a document such as that which follows:

Commonwealth of Australia

Minute Paper
The Director:
Women Trade Commissioners?

Even after some deliberation, it is difficult to find reasons to support the appointment of women Trade Commissioners.

In countries where publicity media is well developed, such as North America and England and where there are no other major drawbacks, such as the Islamic attitude towards women, a relatively young attractive woman could operate with some effectiveness, in a subordinate capacity. As she would probably be the only woman Assistant Trade Commissioner in the whole area, as other countries employ women in this capacity hardly at all, she could attract a measure of interest and publicity.

If we had an important trade in women's clothing and accessories, a woman might promote this more effectively than a man.

Even conceding these points, such an appointee would not stay young and attractive for ever and later on could well become a problem.

It is much easier to find difficulties, some of which spring to mind are: –

1. Women are not employed, except to an extremely minor degree, as career Trade Commissioners in any known service;
2. It is difficult to visualize them as Trade Commissioners, firstly because they could not mix nearly as freely with businessmen as men do. Most men's clubs, for instance, do not allow women members;
3. Relationships with businessmen would tend to be somewhat formal and guarded on both sides. This would make it more difficult for a woman to obtain information;
4. It is extremely doubtful if a woman could, year after year, under a variety of conditions, stand the fairly severe strains and stresses, mentally and physically, which are part of the life of a Trade Commissioner;
5. A man normally has his household run efficiently by his wife, who also looks after much of the entertaining. A woman Trade Commissioner would have all this on top of her normal work;
6. If we engaged single graduates as trainees, most of them would probably marry within five years;
7. If we recruited from the business world, we would have a much smaller field from which to recruit, as the number of women executives in business is quite small;
8. A spinster lady can, and very often does, turn into something of a battleaxe with the passing years. A man usually mellows;

9. A woman would take the place of a man and preclude us from giving practical experience to one male officer. She could marry at any time and be lost to us. She could not be regarded as a long-term investment in the same sense as we regard a man.

Conclusion

It would seem that the noes have it.

A.R. Taysom

13 March 1963

PS I have ascertained the following, which, it would seem, only serves to support the foregoing views:

Mr H.W. Woodruff, UK Trade Commissioner:

They have a few women Trade Commissioners but only in capital city posts, for they have found that women cannot operate where contact with businessmen is necessary.

The women are fairly senior people from the UK Departments and presumably handle trade policy work only.

Mr N. Parkinson, External Affairs:

Since their recruitments of trainees are made under the Public Service Act, there is no way of precluding women from applying and in fact, many more applications are received from women than from men. Some are chosen and all appointments are made on the basis of the quality of their educational achievements. About one woman is appointed to every twelve men. This year one out of sixteen, last year one out of twelve and the previous year, none.

They have to be trained for eighteen months before going to their first post. The average marries within five years.

It is a very expensive process, but External Affairs lack courage to slam the door because of parliamentary opinion, pressure groups and so on.

Worth including? I felt so, as looking back over my career, some of the very best colleagues I have worked with at home and abroad, have been women, for which I shall always be grateful.

So reflecting over thirty-four years with the Trade Commissioner Service, almost all of which was spent overseas, one overriding realisation is the importance of family in one's life. In the final analysis, especially as one gets on in years, family is all that really matters.

The laughter, the tears. The joys, the tragedies. The successes, the failures. The pride felt in one's children's development as wonderfully good human beings, something quite apart from academic and sporting successes, is deeply felt.

In addition are the cherished friendships cemented along the way, with people from so many countries, who have added to our life by letting us into theirs, their minds and homes, their cultures, their values and their aspirations.

We have learned so much along the way.

Close behind all the foregoing is the warmth and gratitude we carry with us, of which there has been no diminution over the years since retirement in 1995. Colleagues and their families – both fellow Trade Commissioners and locally engaged staff – formed a vital part of the operation of Austrade's offices overseas. We do sincerely thank you all. Some are extra special. You know who you are.

What lies ahead?

Having experienced a wide range of societies, their ways, their attitudes to other peoples of different race and religion, I have formed an opinion of the world that is being faced by our children and will be by our grandchildren and beyond. You may not agree, but let me share some thoughts with you.

Faced with life on a planet of finite size and resources, water in particular, and an exponentially increasing population, it has been obvious for some time that pressures over a wide range of essentials are mounting and accelerating.

Whilst human populations increase, those of the animal (land and sea) kingdom are facing increased exploitation, and, in some cases, extinction. I am of course referring to native species that will disappear because of loss of habitat e.g. orangutans, as a result of forests being cleared to be replaced by palm oil plantations, or other human activity, e.g. killing of elephants for their tusks. Man's priorities will prevail – the clearing of land for crops and raising of domestic animals to meet the demand of increasing populations, seemingly evades any solution.

The necessity of maintaining an adequate food, water and already finite mineral supply, together with man's greed, are also seemingly unreachable without affecting other species sharing this planet.

On the matter of climate change, particularly global warming, sceptics would say, at the very least, that the jury is still out. Others often stridently proclaim that there is no evidence that a long-term trend to a permanent change in climate can be successfully argued.

Personally, I believe enough evidence exists to suggest that very real problems face those (human and animal) who wish to continue to inhabit planet Earth.

Solutions are and will be very difficult to devise, but the reality must be faced that we do live on a planet of finite resources – water and energy in particular – and that insofar as energy is concerned, future demands will only be met if nuclear power is included in the generation of electricity equation. Power from solar, wind and wave will never meet the base load demands of the future. The 'greens' will vehemently disagree, but in doing so, they are only, as did the ostrich, burying their heads in the sand.

Obviously there are pressing problems of an immediate nature that need urgent addressing. The inability and/or unwillingness of national governments or world bodies to face up to these problems is both evident and, to me anyway, of great concern. They present an impediment at the least, and a huge problem at the worst, to the achievement of global harmony.

Those of an immediate nature, what are they? I believe that there are two in particular – quite apart from those associated with the climate change and water resources issues debate.

The first is that of corruption. Its influence in all facets of most, at least many, governments and world economies, and indeed the daily lives of millions, is obvious. They range from the activities of drug cartels to leaders of nations who build 'palaces' for themselves and their supporters, whilst their peoples starve, or at best live very miserable lives.

The second is the inability of some peoples to even try to live with each other, often because of deep-rooted customs. In so many of the trouble spots of the world today, societies are fiercely tribal in nature. They have been for centuries. This is further complicated by overriding religious divisions. Throughout history there have been many examples of savage conflicts as a result of religious divide. Anti-Semitic attitudes and actions require no elaboration.

However, in those past eras conflicts were contained to much smaller regions or issues. Could be one tribe against another over authority as to ownership of a particular desert area or even an insult made to a leader of one tribe by one of another.

Today we witness conflicts of ideas involving so many and causing so much suffering. Whole generations of children have, and are, growing up knowing nothing other than war. Many will never receive an education. The effect on their minds and future actions as they grow is of great concern. Palestinian versus Israeli has been an issue in the modern era since 1948. Of even greater concern involves divisions within those professing Islam as their faith, and here the numbers are daunting. Sunni versus Shiite. Did the war in Iraq to oust Saddam Hussein achieve anything? Absolutely not. The killings continue. The Saddam repressive Sunni regime over the more populous Shiites once ended has seen a Shiite government seize power, which clearly is Shiite first and Iraqi a distant second. The tit for tat bombings and killings will continue. I would add, that a major contributory factor to this ongoing situation in Iraq has been that of disbanding the Iraqi army by the United States at the end of the war. A trained, disciplined body of men and women, who could have been redirected to maintain discipline.

A similar situation exists throughout many countries bordering the Mediterranean.

At the partition of India we witnessed Muslim pitted against Hindu. Absolute carnage before the separate states of Pakistan (East and West) were carved off from the previously colonial rule of India as a whole. East Pakistan subsequently became the independent state of Bangladesh.

This second major problem is of greater concern and present indications are that it is almost unsolvable if left to the leaders of countries most involved.

Perhaps in the not too distant future it will rest with China or India to be the arbitrator? Now there's a thought!

A comment on the often controversial subject of Aboriginal conciliation. First, there is certain evidence that early settlement by Europeans, particularly British settlers – free men and women and convicts – inflicted what today would be seen as misdeeds demanding trials in The Hague. Justified at the time by these early immigrants, because of the 'Terra Nullius Australis' designation of this new land – no human beings existed! Outrageous!

Denial of the right to vote and the Stolen Generations, the forced removal of children from their mothers to be brought up in the ways of the white man, are just two examples of the treatment of an indigenous people that will forever remain a dark stain on our society.

However, whilst never forgetting, we citizens of this great country must move forward. The official apology has been made and accepted, words can do no more. Political correctness has in many instances been taken to an extreme. Any criticism is usually labelled racist and leapt upon by the press, politicians and others with positions of influence. This must change if we are indeed to move forward.

A big part of this necessity has to be the delivery to many indigenous communities throughout Australia, those services to meet massive needs in the improvement of living standards, to combat alcoholism, to improve health and education, in fact in almost all those basic rights to which they are entitled.

However, and this is the main point I wish to make, is that the delivery of these necessary services must be carried out by indigenous persons and not by white officials. They will of course require training and a process of selection to fill these positions needs to be implemented. To have government money thrown at needy communities has been shown to be at best, ineffective, and at worst, destructive.

Finally, on the emotive subject of how we, as a country, so enriched by settlers from so many distant lands, deal with those we refer to as 'refugees', 'boat people', 'illegal immigrants', whatever.

We are dealing with human beings. In many instances we treat these men, women and children as animals. A disgrace. If the decision has to be made, hopefully never again, that Australia has to send men and women to war, that decision is not made by a left or a right faction, but by a partisan government of elected members. Again, we are dealing with human beings, MOST of whom have anguished over the decision as to whether to leave their own country (they desperately wish they didn't have to), and to do so, have not only had to use all of their life's savings, but many have had to borrow large sums of money.

The administration of refugees once they reach our shores should be carried out with a bipartisan approach and not a public slanging match between various political parties. They MUST have their claims to refugee status handled expeditiously. Months of being left in limbo behind wire is simply unacceptable, and, sadly, this has been the situation faced by refugees for many years. We, as a rich and free nation, should be ashamed of ourselves, particularly given that the numbers involved are a fraction of those that almost all other developed countries have to deal with.

So, as the words of the well-known song go (to those of my age anyway!) 'the party's over, it's time to call it a day …' I leave you with a warm thank you, to all who have enriched the lives of Maureen and myself and that of our family.

Wakefield Press is an independent publishing and
distribution company based in Adelaide, South Australia.
We love good stories and publish beautiful books.
To see our full range of books, please visit our website at
www.wakefieldpress.com.au
where all titles are available for purchase.

Find us!

Twitter: www.twitter.com/wakefieldpress
Facebook: www.facebook.com/wakefield.press
Instagram: instagram.com/wakefieldpress